From Price Tag

To

Priceless

Adriana Ivett Petty

Copyright © 2015 by Adriana Ivett Petty

All rights reserved.

ISBN-13:9781519464309
ISBN-10:1519464304

Edited by Erin Buckingham

The stories you will read in this book are for illustrative examples not based on specific events or people.

Hoopre

You are Precious - Beloved
and only you can do what you were
created to do!
          XO XL XO

2016

This book is dedicated to all of you amazing ladies; may you rip off the price tag and realize how precious and priceless you truly are!

Acknowledgments

Writing this book would not have been possible without the love and support from the following key individuals in my life. Joseph Lee Petty, my husband: I do not believe I would have written this book if it were not for you. Thank you for your unending encouragement and great conversations, which led to writing this book. I am eternally grateful for your love and transparency and for challenging me to never settle or get too comfortable.

I would like to also thank my family; you all mean so much to me. My parents, Angela Garces and Guadalupe Garces, and my in-laws, Viola and Hezikah Petty, thank you for your love and support. I am also grateful for my siblings, Jose and Julie Garces as well as Hezikah Petty and Annie and Roger Cotton. To the next generation that will branch out and take our family legacy to new levels: Mercedes, Vincent, Lexus, Angel, and Julian Garces, as well as Matthew, Rishod, Jessica, Josiah, and Jelani Cotton, and Jaylen Knapp-Petty. I love all of you so much!

    Thank you, Bertha Carson King and Danielle Minnes, two special friends whom read, from beginning to end, various versions of my manuscript. Thank you for your time, input, and encouragement.

    I would especially like to thank Erin Buckingham, my editor. This book would not be what it is today without your eminent skill. Thank you for performing your task so beautifully.

    Most importantly, I want to thank You, for loving me when I felt unlovable. You forgave me when I messed up, and You were always there for me, even when I was trying to run away. Thank you for embracing me when I came back to You; just as I was, You loved me. You cleaned me up and made me like new. Though I did not feel worthy of Your love, You gave it to me anyway. Thank you for not only loving me this way, but for also offering Your love, mercy, and grace to anyone willing to receive it. Thank you, my Lord and Savior Jesus Christ; there is no greater love than Yours.

Table of Contents

Introduction

Chapter One: Categories - 1

Chapter Two: Main - 8

Chapter Three: 2nd - 15

Chapter Four: 3rd - 22

Chapter Five: Mirror, Mirror On The Wall - 33

Chapter Six: The Girl Program - 53

Chapter Seven: Boys Play Games, - 73
Girls Play Pretend

Chapter Eight: Fooled By A Feeling - 92

Chapter Nine: Courtship VS. Dating - 99

Chapter Ten: Finders Keepers - 114

Chapter Eleven: Bonus Nuggets - 120
- Lie VS. Omission
- Monogamy
- Right Person Wrong Time
- Price Tag VS. Priceless
- Subcategories

Chapter Twelve: Wives - 184

Chapter Thirteen: Conclusion ~ My Story - 191

From Price Tag To Priceless

Introduction

I sat in my car, unable to speak. I couldn't believe what I had just heard. While I was trying to process what he said, my sight grew blurry. I was so relieved that we were doing this over the phone, that he couldn't see how much his words were affecting me. I closed my eyes, and I felt the tears roll down my cheeks. We were over – again. But this time was different. I was done with this relationship rollercoaster. We started out as friends, but now, after everything we had been through, I just didn't want to be his friend. Throughout the five years we were involved, I had been categorized and re-categorized by him. Now it was time for me to discover and redefine myself. By redefining myself I was then re-categorized. It wasn't until I was able to understand my self value that I was able to metaphorically rip off the tags others had placed on me and realize how precious and priceless I really am.

This process of learning and then understanding my self-value was not a quick transition; it took time and effort. But it was so worth it! It still takes effort to unlearn and undo negative, unattainable, unrealistic patterns of thinking and acting. Growing up, I was bombarded with messages of love and happily ever after. Think about it, how many times would you guess that you have received a message about romantic love? And by message I mean: heard stories of people falling in love, listened to a song pertaining to love, or watched a movie about a love story? In my lifetime, I really couldn't even guess the number of times this message has been apparent. I was introduced to the idea of romantic love at a young age. I, like many little girls, was read fairytales, bible stories, fables, and short stories about love. I also watched a lot of cartoons that were either about a love story or at least had some kind of romantic story within the cartoon. As I got older, I read romantic novels and repeatedly watched romantic movies.

When a song comes on now, I know the movie it was featured in, and I am able to quote a sappy line from the movie. You would think that with this much inundation of this topic in my life, whether intentional or not, I would have been able to have had a successful and healthy love life. That was certainly not the case! I, like many others, put myself through terrible heartaches. It wasn't until I took the time to really look at myself that I was able to heal and then to identify and accept real love. My purpose for writing about this topic is to provide a new resource that will demonstrate the importance of understanding self-value, to better equip you for love.

  I know that there are several resources available that present the topic of love produced by both men and women. However, with every resource, you really have to be a detective to clearly see the author's agenda. Because the author's agenda will influence your choices, it is important that you know up front whether this new resource will help you or hurt you. So here's a little about me and my agenda:

As I said above, I had been introduced to the topic of romantic love through books, songs, and films. But the relationships I saw growing up were nothing like the ones in the books, films, or songs. I didn't have any examples of healthy, mature, and loving relationships. I had two conflicting perspectives of love: healthy vs. unhealthy or happy vs. unhappy. Why was the depiction of love in all of the songs, stories, and films so different than what I saw in real life? And why was it that when I had the opportunity to experience this beautiful thing called love, I ended up in heartache? Why, when I had all of this research, resources, and examples of happily ever after, was I more broken than when I started?

After going through my experiences, it is my desire to merely present the "blueprint". By explaining this layout and the different positions, I hope to provide you with some insight into the age-old situation of dating. Looking at the familiar through a different angle, you will be able to identify patterns of choices and their consequences. By knowing these patterns and consequences, you will be able to look at what you have been doing and decide if you want to maintain your current path or choose to make changes to improve your situation.

As a reformed romantic, I know firsthand what happens when the "storytelling" begins: attention becomes selective. You may have heard the term "selective hearing". When it comes to the topic of romance, women tend to have, what I am coining as, "selective connection". This is how this works: You hear a story about how two people came together and are now happy. As you are listening to their story, you selectively choose to connect to certain elements that are familiar or personal to you. These elements that you choose to connect with can be as minimal as they met at a grocery store that you frequent and already you have made a connection. In your mind you are already preparing to be sure to take a little bit more time putting yourself together before going to that particular store because of this connection that you have made. If someone has met their "Mr. Right" while they shopped at the same store where you shop, then it might also happen to you.

We hear stories all the time about how two people met and fell in love, but what we don't hear are all the elements that were in place to get to that point. We don't know the struggles, the mundane aspects of their day-to-day situation that all feed into their relationship. We don't know their communication styles, how they handle conflict, or what past baggage they are bringing into the new relationship. There are all of these unknown details, and, yet, most women want to hear about a happy ending and want that for themselves. We are so accustomed to selectively connecting to a few of the elements in the story and at times miss the parts that we really should have paid more attention to. As you read along, there will be information and scenarios to demonstrate the different points. However, the scenarios will be brief and may leave you wanting to hear more of the situation. Because I don't want to lose you in the story, they will be cut short. Oh, and just a word of caution: after you read the scenarios, don't try to over analyze what you have just read.

    I desire to layout the situation from a different perspective, not to provide a beautiful atmosphere to get lost in. It's time to stop getting lost and instead really find *you*. Once you find yourself, it will be a lot harder to lose yourself in a relationship that causes more pain than love. Real and true love doesn't cause harm. This doesn't mean that you won't get hurt from time to time, but there should be no cause for harm when you are dealing with real love.

From Price Tag To Priceless

Chapter One – Categories

Remember that old saying, "why buy the cow when you can get the milk for free?" As old fashioned as that saying is, men still believe in this saying and other similar beliefs when they are choosing a woman to be in a relationship with. When it comes to committing to someone, a man has standards of what he wants in a wife. He has a rating system that determines the women that meet his standards. All men have a rating system. Many men categorize women within 15 minutes of meeting. Whether or not women are aware of their position, they are, at that moment, being categorized. And for different men, the same woman can fall under a different category. Not all women maintain the category they are initially given. Many women may start off in one category but, with time, they may be "reclassified". These categories (Main, 2nd, and 3rd) define how a man will label and treat you, and how he will talk to other men about you.

Categories: Main, 2nd, and 3rd

To Identify Main, 2nd, and 3rd here is a quick definition to better see each category:

- Main – wife material, girlfriend material, and trophy girl

- 2nd – "emotional girlfriend", at times a girlfriend, and is a person that a man tends to call to talk about his dreams and future; a best friend kind of role and many times mostly platonic

- 3rd – "booty call" the person a man calls for a quick fix then leaves; there is usually an arrangement that it's just sex with no strings attached and sleeping over is optional but not common

These are very basic definitions of the categories, but as you continue to read on, you will see that the categorization of women can become very complex.

<u>Why is it important to know the categories?</u>

Through the years, I've seen countless relationships start and end and have witnessed the painful turmoil people go through. I've seen women wounded from heartache "emotionally" crawl away from the relationship, then see them repeat the same pattern over and over again. The earlier she would start dating, the more lost she would be by the time she was in her 20's. This pattern became more detrimental the longer she stayed on this path until she finally looked back and examined her past relationships.

It's not until we stop, step back and look at our past that we can start to see our patterns. It's not until the pattern is identified that it can be addressed and changed. But knowing our pattern is not enough. You can't solve a problem by merely looking at it from one angle; it's important to really study it. So, once you know your pattern, it's important to know the other side, the men's side – the categories.

Categorization

Knowledge of this rating system has been around a long time and has not been kept a secret, yet women turn a blind eye to it and ultimately endure more hurt and heartache than necessary. These types of codes or rating systems are weaved into old clichés. "Why by the cow when the milk's for free" still rings very true in how many men think, and women should pay more attention to this and other similar sayings.

Rating or labeling women goes back a long way. Even in the Bible you can find examples of women being categorized. The only difference between then and now is that there are a slew of new words created to label women. In the Bible, some women are described as 'virtuous' and 'harlot/whore'. Some of the current words that are now used are words such as 'wifey' and 'chicken-head'. But all of these words, old and new, were created with one purpose: to determine a woman's worth and to categorize her. Men use these labels to separate women and to treat them according to how they categorize them. Doing so allows men to decide how involved they will become with each type of woman and the level of responsibility they have towards them.

While men are the ones that categorize women, it's the women that ultimately determine the category they will be in. In order to change her category, she must face some hard facts.

The Facts:

1) You are treated the way you allow others to treat you

2) The kind of person you want to be with may not be the kind of person you need to be with

3) You may say you want to know the truth but are unwilling to face/see the truth

4) You are afraid to be lonely/alone

5) You may only be fulfilled in one area of a relationship and can't help but feel a void that you can't explain

6) You have a nagging feeling that something is off in your relationship: there is something off about your relationship

7) You ask men the wrong questions

8) You are either oblivious to your category or in denial of it

Unless you are willing to face these hard facts, your situation won't change. You will still have that small voice in the back of your mind telling you that something is off. You will still have that knot in your stomach wondering why things aren't better. The void will continue to be there. Your short fuse will continue to get shorter. There may be a quiet acceptance, a type of surrender, that this is as good as it will get and try to ignore that yearning inside of you.

From Price Tag To Priceless

Chapter Two - Main

The Main is, at first glance, the position most women want. But looks can be deceiving. A characteristic of a Main is that she is the woman that catches a man's eye because of how she looks and the initial impression she makes on him. There is something about her that draws people's attention.

At first glance, the Main looks as if it's all going to work out for her, and she will be in a committed relationship and happy. However, it doesn't always work out that way. Let's say that a man spots an attractive woman that fits his qualifications for a Main and they go out. During the date, he begins to investigate to see if she really is all that he wants her to be. Then, BOOM – he sees something and instantly re-categorizes her. She still might be Main material, but now she is no longer 'wife' material because she is now a part of a Main-subcategory.

Confusing? Yes. To make this a bit more clear, let's get into the Main-subcategory.

The Trophy

This subcategory is pretty self-explanatory. What happens is that a man will be attracted to a woman thinking that she's his perfect Main based on how she looks. Once he investigates her, he finds that there is something lacking, and she goes from being a Main (and a strong girlfriend to possibly wife material) over to a Trophy girl. So what is lacking that took her out of the running of becoming his future wife? Well, it can be a number of things like:

- She's not smart enough
- She doesn't have a sense of humor
- She's too eager (to have sex, a boyfriend, a husband. Basically, she moves too fast or wants too much)
- She has a lot of guy friends
- She's too independent (makes him feel like she doesn't need/want him)

- She doesn't have a nice laugh (yes, I know it's shallow but if a guy hears a girl laugh and doesn't like it, he will try to put up with it, then when it becomes too much, he's out)

- She's not about anything/doesn't aspire to much

- She's too materialistic

- She's too or not enough physically active

- She doesn't have enough in common with him

- She has a bad attitude (stuck-up, unkind, or ungrateful)

- She's selfish

Once a man re-classifies a woman as a Trophy instead of a Main, then he will take her out to be seen with her and show her off. What he is really doing is showing others the kind of girl he can get. He shows her off and then breaks-up with her. He earns a lot of points for showing that he could get a girl that looked like that and was able to "not want her" and cast her aside for someone he considers better. Note: Both men and women notice when a man has a beautiful girl. It makes these other women wonder what the man has to offer because he is clearly able to get such a beautiful woman, and they become open to finding out for themselves.

Going from Main to Trophy girl isn't the only option. A Main can also become re-categorized as a 3rd due to her actions. A Main becomes a 3rd by being too eager to be with him. When he realizes that she wants him, it is easy for him to define the parameters of when, where, and why he wants to see her. If these encounters (not dates) are sexual early on, it quickly results in the woman going from Main to 3rd. Let's face it, if you don't think you're worth waiting for, then why would he find you valuable? Why would he place or see more value in you than you do for yourself?

<u>Warning, Warning, Warning</u>

Mains, if you are "marriage material" and men aren't jumping at the chance to be with you, there is a perfectly good reason: they aren't ready to settle down. As a result, a lot of Mains end up boyfriend-less/dateless. You see, a man doesn't want to ruin the opportunity to be with a good woman when he knows he's not ready to settle down. With that in mind, he keeps the Main close enough to know what she is doing and makes her his 'friend'. This leads us to a new Main subcategory, the Main/2nd. One con to being a Main/2nd is that she will see men approaching other women around her and not approach her. Do not despair if you are a Main/2nd that keeps getting overlooked. The best thing to do is to continue to live by your standards. It may not be the most exciting journey when the girls are talking about their latest relationship and you feel you don't have anything to contribute to the conversation. Usually, the women that have the most to contribute are the ones experiencing the most heartbreak and emptiness. You aren't missing out on anything worth having. Fill your time with things and activities that you enjoy and work on accomplishing your dreams. Until "Mr. Right" comes and finds you, have fun discovering who you are and live a fulfilling life. By doing that, you don't lose.

Main Self-Assessment (qualities of a Main)

- Meet friends of the man you are dating
- Meet family of the man you are dating
- He introduces you as his "Girlfriend"
- He takes you on dates during the Morning, Noon, and Evening
- He is eager about introducing you to the people he knows
- He picks you up to take you to his family/friend functions
- He invites you to do the things he likes to do/hobbies
- He talks to you about his aspirations, dreams, future plans
- He includes you in his future plans *you, specifically, note that he is specifically talking about you and not just someone in general*
- He takes an interest in your likes/hobbies and participates in some of them with you
- He meets your friends and family

- He attends your family/friend/work functions
- He talks to you on the phone regularly
- He goes to see you regularly
- He takes you out to public places – no place is off limits
- He talks to you about his family, his past, and his hopes for the future
- He tells you what you mean to him
- He is very open about himself to you
- Pays when on dates

From Price Tag To Priceless

Chapter Three - 2nd

You know those cliché movies where the girl is secretly in love with her best friend and the guy is usually busy in love with another girl. Then she helps him to train up to be able to ask the other girl out. In most of those movies, eventually, the guy sees the girl that has been right in front of his face the whole time. He sees that she is the one he really wants to be with. Sometimes it takes some miraculous makeover that involves trading glasses for contacts, a new hair-do, and a change in wardrobe. Or he realizes that he wants his friend when she is no longer available. Other times it takes her to confess what she has been hiding from him, her love, to help him realize that he loves her, too.

You know why those movies are so popular? Because they are true. It often takes an event, something to help the man see the woman in a different way than he has been seeing her when all the while she's been right in front of him.

If you are not in a committed relationship, then 2nd is the ideal place or position to have. As a 2nd, your primary role is being a good friend. A man will always remember a woman that he had a great time with that didn't involve sex. It is important for him to find someone he can really be himself with. When thinking about being married for the rest of your life, why wouldn't you choose to spend it with your best friend? A man doesn't like the thought of losing his 2nd, she's too important to him.

As a 2nd, take advantage of the amount of time you spend with him by getting to know him. Learn what his goals are. How does he handle disappointment? What does he value and believe in? How does he overcome anger? What has he accomplished? Learning about him helps you in two ways: you get to find out if he is the kind of person you want to be with and it helps him form an attachment to you by being so interested in getting to know him. Men like talking about themselves just as much, or maybe even more, than women do.

Sand Trap of a 2nd – don't get stuck

A word of caution: 2^{nd}s often times are overlooked because of falling into certain 'sand traps'. These can all be seen in the movies mentioned above, but I will list them to make them clear.

First is being too comfortable. He comes over and sees you too many times looking frumpy. He may be used to just popping by your place unannounced, and you look like you were not expecting male visitors. Now, I don't mean that when he tells you he's coming over that you run and put on your old prom dress, but at least put on clean clothes that fit instead of your comfy, oversized sweats or pajamas with the worn out t-shirt that is so soft and faded from being washed so much. So, if he gives you a heads up that he's stopping by, wash your face, brush your hair, put on clean clothes that fit so that it doesn't look like you just rolled out of bed.

Second is becoming a doormat. Don't let your friendship/relationship be all about him. Be sure to talk about you and your goals and dreams in conversations. Don't allow yourself to just become a dumping ground for him to stop by, make his deposit of saying all he wants to say, and then get up and leave. If all you do is allow him to talk about himself, he won't ever learn about you. If he doesn't really know you, then why would he take you into consideration when he wonders about who he wants to be with? When you spend time together talking, talk about yourself and what you want to accomplish in your lifetime.

Third is stop being available to him 24/7. Being too available to him is not good either. Don't cancel plans to be available to him. He needs to know that other people enjoy spending time with you. He has to know that he doesn't get all access to you when he wants to. Make plans with your other friends and enjoy yourself. Don't forget if he and you aren't dating then you're still on the market. It's okay for you to go on dates or mention that one of your girlfriends is setting you up on a date. It will peak his interest to know that you are going out because he will be threatened at the thought that you might not be available to him. Making yourself less available to him doesn't mean making yourself available sexually to other men. If you begin having sex with men that you are not in a committed relationship with, it will cause him to re-categorize you.

Being a 2nd, it is key that your relationship stay strictly platonic-no sex! Having sex totally complicates things because, if you have sex while you are a 2nd, it makes it too easy to fall into the 3rd category. After having sex once, it makes it too convenient to do it again. All the while there is no commitment, which leads to the 3rd category. Just say no! If you have a slip up, make it clear that you aren't into that, and it won't happen again.

It's important to really be yourself as a friend/2nd. Don't try to be impressive to the point that you are not being yourself because then you are just misrepresenting yourself. Be true to who you are and know that you are enough.

2nd Self-Assessment (qualities of a 2nd)

- He meets with you privately, most likely in your own home or in very casual public places like coffee shops

- He rarely introduces you to people unless you happen to run into someone while out

- Outings are very platonic: you meet in places rather than get picked up, locations are somewhat limited to your home, cafes, library, etc-basically, locations he is not likely going to run into his friends - and he never calls them dates

- He talks about his future plans and issues he's had with past relationships

- If out and you do run into people he knows, if he chooses to introduce you, he does so in the following manner "This is…" or "This is my friend…" - very platonic

- He may invest a regular amount of time in your friendship; he may talk to you once a week

- He will be interested in your relationships as well and ask if you are seeing anyone, wanting to know your own history with men, asking about why your past relationships haven't worked out (he does this for a very important reason: he's interviewing you)

- He will tend to pay you compliments and encourage you

- He often portrays himself in the best possible light; many times you will hear the sob stories of how he has been wronged in the past or how he was the victim in situations
- There is no sex

- You find yourself talking about him to your friends

- Your friends tend to ask why you and he haven't started dating, which gives you more to think about

- When you are out, he pays for himself

From Price Tag To Priceless

Chapter Four - 3rd

The most painful situation I put myself through was deciding to become a 3rd. If I would have known what being a 3rd entailed and the consequences of being a 3rd, I would not have done it. I was seeing a guy for a few months, and then he told me that he didn't want to be in a relationship anymore.

    I saw him soon after we were no longer together and decided to talk to him. To be honest, I really didn't want him to think or know that he had hurt me. I made the first move. I walked up to him and greeted him casually and as carefree as possible. I had a lot of fun when I hung out with him, so it was easy to spend time with him. Quickly, we decided to "just be friends". And just as quickly we became "friends with benefits". BAM, there it is, I was now a 3rd. Very quickly, I went from girlfriend, to friend, to friend with benefits. Or, a Main, to a 2nd, to a 3rd.

As a girlfriend, I understood that he was my plus-one, the person I was intimate with. We went on dates and he paid. He would drive over to pick me up and take me out. He introduced me to his family and friends. As his girlfriend, I knew my role and his.

When we became 'friends' (after having been boyfriend/girlfriend) our relationship was a bit complicated. You see, with my other male friends, there wasn't the same kind of flirtation as with him. I cared about how I looked when I knew that we would see each other, even though we were just friends. There were a lot of double meanings or sexual innuendos in our conversations. We even gave each other advice on what to do in our future hypothetical relationships. Our relationship as friends was very easy, which shouldn't be surprising because of our past connection. It was because of being able to enjoy each other's company that we began to date in the first place.

Being friends was easy; the difficult part was to restrain ourselves to only being friends.

It was while we were hanging out as friends that we crossed the friendship line and became intimate, thus becoming friends with benefits. Of course, deciding to do this was preceded with hypothetical conversations. The thing is, he told me he didn't want to be in a monogamous relationship, but he enjoyed being with me. If I would have decided to listen to what he said and asked myself a few questions and answered them honestly, I would have made a better choice for myself and saved myself from a lot of unnecessary hurt.

So, these are the questions I should have asked myself when he said he didn't want to be in a monogamous relationship:

- Do I want to be with someone (sexually) who wants to have sex with other women?
- Do I want to share a man with other women?

- Do I want to entrust myself (body and heart) to someone who doesn't want to be in a committed relationship with me?

- Why would I want to be with someone who doesn't want to be with only me?

If I would have taken the time to ask myself these simple questions and realized the simple answers, I would have known that this was the time to cut my losses and remove myself from the situation. But no, that's not what I did. Instead of listening to what he said, I listened to how I felt. When we were together, he made me feel like I was the only one, even though he clearly said he didn't want to be in a monogamous relationship. I went on what I felt, instead of what I knew. When I found out that he had been with another woman, I would be upset and feel betrayed. Again, he clearly told me that he did not want to be in a monogamous relationship.

I continued to be in this situation for a while, and it was always the same. I would answer the phone when he called. He would invite me over to his house to watch a movie or have dinner. We would hang out and then eventually end up having sex. Then I would leave, and he would call me again, and we would repeat our encounters. This went on pretty smoothly until I would find out about him being with someone else. Then I would get mad and confront him, he would remind me of how we weren't in a committed relationship, and I would leave crying and hurt. Then he would call, I would answer, and we would do it all over again.

By writing out our dysfunctional cycle, it is clear to see how to get off the merry-go-round of hurt because it looks very clear cut and dry – stop answering the phone. The problem was what I chose to believe, see, and hear instead of what he said from the beginning. He said "I don't want to be in a monogamous relationship". He never changed his stance. What he did do was redefine our relationship. He wanted to be able to date and have sex with anyone he wanted to without having to explain himself or answer to anyone about it.

Now, for some people, having this kind of 'I got mine, you got yours' arrangement works. They can maintain this type of situation without wanting more. I get how it can work temporarily for some people. If you went through a traumatic divorce or break-up and want your sexual needs met but aren't ready to open yourself to someone, this arrangement might work, temporarily. The problem was that this kind of situation was not one that I could handle. I didn't know how to not want more. I wanted a relationship. I wasn't comfortable playing games because I actually wanted real love. I didn't know how to only have sex. The kicker was even when I thought I could handle it and tried it, I wasn't doing it the right way. You see, I was with only him, whereas, he dealt with several women.

The Double Standard

Repeat after me: in relationships, there's always a double standard - always! In this situation, it was that he could see and have sex with whomever he wanted but, it was a problem for him if I was seeing or having sex with someone else. To demonstrate how this worked I will give you a very painful example. One night he tells me that he's been seeing a woman who had children (he always had said that he didn't want to be involved with a woman with children, too much responsibility). I knew that we were over. He wanted to be in a relationship with her and he was even breaking one of his own rules to be with her. So I started hanging out with another guy who he knew (not my greatest moment). One night I'm at a club and a drunk friend of his comes over to me and starts to berate me and tries to make me feel ashamed for seeing the other guy. Now, he may or may not have known that the difference between what we did was that he was having sex with the other woman before he told me that he wanted to be in a relationship with her. Whereas I started seeing the new guy after being 'let go' and had not had sex with him. But it didn't matter; in his eyes, I was the wrong one. Double standard. Quickly, my name was being smeared, not only amongst his male friends but also his female friends who always waited for me to make a mistake. You see, he knew that he had been doing me wrong for some time, and he could not wait to prove that I wasn't as perfect as people may have thought I had been.

After making several bad decisions, I finally came to my senses and washed my hands of both of them. It felt a bit too coincidental to be coincidence, like one would call after the other. It was then that I decided to not deal with either of them. I had a choice to make. I could jump down the rabbit hole of immediate self-gratification and from man to man who happened to pay me a nice compliment that made me feel validated as a woman, or I could take some time out and work on myself. I chose the latter. I cried a lot and then got myself to church to reprioritize myself. I focused on becoming the kind of person that I wanted to be. I wanted to someday be someone's wife. I wanted to someday be in love with a man who really loved me and only me.

We all have our reasons for why we accept less than what we really want. But, in the end, hopefully, we see that we deserve to have what we want and are willing to work towards it. This is what I encourage you to do. Stop settling for what a man says he is willing to give you. If you want a committed relationship and the man tells you that he doesn't, believe him and move on to someone who does want what you want, with you. Don't waste your time, energy, or tears on someone who isn't willing to treat and love you the way you deserve to be loved.

Sometimes it is hard to see the truth, so I have to ask the question, are you being labeled or treated as a 3rd?

Below are some ways to make it easier to see the kind of treatment a 3rd receives.

3rd Self – Assessment (qualities of a 3rd)

- He calls for booty calls/casual sex late at night
- His friends tend to try and talk to you as well – flirting with you
- He might introduce you to some of his guy friends, especially if he met you in a club
- You rarely meet his friends/family, and, if you do, it is a very casual introduction
- Usually, you end up meeting at locations, not driving together
- He doesn't make a great effort to see you during holidays
- He doesn't remember your birthday unless you remind him
- He doesn't make any commitments to you
- He only pays for himself, doesn't offer to pay for you
- He won't explain himself to you – he does not feel he owes you anything

- If questioned about your relationship and where it is headed, he gets frustrated/annoyed/angry and says something like "I already told you what I want, that hasn't changed"

If you are being treated this way and want it to change, then *you* have to change. Make it clear what you want, and, if it is not what he wants, you can walk away from that relationship. Stop answering his calls and stop accommodating him. Redirect your energy and time on yourself. Focus on what you want and how to get there. Surround yourself with happy friends. This is key! Why? Because, if you surround yourself with friends who will encourage you to 'get yours' or to get even, the only thing you have changed is that you are being a 3rd to more men. The goal is not to be someone else's 3rd but to be someone's one and only. Happy people don't waste their time and energy worrying about if other people are watching them look happy; they are too busy being happy to care if anyone is noticing.

From Price Tag To Priceless

Chapter Five - Mirror, Mirror On The Wall

Women and men think, interpret, and then respond differently yet parallel to one another. Men tend to approach a situation from a logical perspective: address the issue, then it's finished. Women tend to approach a situation from an analytical perspective: address the issue, observe the outcome, question and reflect if the issue was resolved the best possible way, and file the issue away to be pulled back up if needed at a later date. The fact that we process information differently yet in a parallel way causes many complications when dealing with relationships.

By looking in the mirror and really seeing the reflection, instead of seeing what we want to see, we can better examine ourselves and identify things that need to change to better our situation. Earlier, I listed some hard truths and will now address each of them.

1) You are treated the way you allow others to treat you

If you are in a relationship and are not being treated in a way that you feel you should be treated, the first thing to do is address the situation. First, think about your relationship. What about the way you are treated in the relationship bothers you? Make a list of the things that bother you about your treatment. Taking the time to write these things down on paper makes you conscious and aware about how you are allowing yourself to be treated. A reason that this is important is that when you feel that you are in love with a person, it is easy to make excuses for their shortcomings. Until you are willing to become conscious of the things that bother you, you'll allow yourself to let them continue to bother you. Because of how you feel towards them, you excuse being let down. However, you keep the feelings about the situation 'filed away' until you choose to remember them (usually when you're not happy with the person). To better identify areas that you would like to address, complete the following statements:

- I don't feel appreciated when…
- It upsets me when…
- I would rather…
- It hurts my feelings when…
- I don't feel respected when…
- It is important to me that…

After you have completed the above statements, look at them and see what it is you feel. You can also consider and answer the following questions:

- Do you feel that you are being heard?
- Do you feel you are being respected?
    - If not, how specifically do you feel disrespected?
- Are your feelings being valued?
    - If not, how are they being devalued?
- How accommodating are you in the relationship?

- How much does your partner accommodate you?

- How much time have you invested in the relationship?
    - Is it equal or close to the amount that your partner invests in the relationship?

- How much money have you invested into a relationship?
    - Is it equal or close to the amount that your partner invests in the relationship?

- Do you tend to call the person more than the person calls you?

- The activities that you do when you are together
    - Are they things that he likes to do or things you like to do?

By starting this process of thinking about your relationship, you are able to see it as it is verses how it started out being or how you would like it to be. After you have written down the things that bother you about how you are treated in a relationship, really reflect on what you have written. This is key because these are the things that you have to choose whether or not they are worth either working through or ending a relationship.

Now it's time to address the issues you have with how you have been treated in a relationship. It is very important that you don't go into the discussion in attack mode but instead have a calm and clear conversation. He may not know that he hurt your feelings or hurt you because you had not made it clear before. It's very important that you address the issues you have in a logical way versus an emotional way. If you become emotional, you could risk the person not hearing you because you are not being clear about what is bothering you or what you want changed. After you have said what you needed to say, then you have to listen to his response. This could be a turning point in the relationship. He may apologize not realizing that you felt the way you felt.

If he dismisses your request for better treatment, then the cards are in your hands. You have to decide if you want to be with a person that is not willing to give you what you feel you need to continue to be invested in the relationship. If they are not willing to change, are you willing to leave? It may sound harsh, but why would you stay in a relationship in which you are not treated well? How much of your time are you willing to invest in a relationship that does not provide you with the kind of treatment you feel you deserve?

2) The kind of person you want to be with may not be the kind of person you need to be with

The issue of want verses need can be a complicated and difficult issue for a person to be completely honest with themselves about. Looking at want versus need makes a person ask the question 'why'. Why are you attracted to a person? What, from your history are you trying to reconcile with in your present?

To better see want versus need, and how past hurt can affect a person in the present, here is an example: Daisy had been dating Ethan for two years. He told her that he wasn't ready to be in a committed relationship and wanted to see other people. Daisy had very strong feelings for

Ethan and thought she could handle an open relationship. She didn't date other men while he dated other women. When Daisy found out about Ethan dating other women, she felt hurt and confronted Ethan. He always reminded her that he had told her from the beginning that he was not ready for a committed relationship and that he would date other people. Daisy opened up to her sister about what was happening and her sister asked her why she wanted to be committed to someone who didn't want to be committed to her.

    Daisy responded, "Why am I not enough? Why does he have to see other women?" Her sister shook her head and said, "You're just like mom." Her sister's response struck Daisy. She started to think about how her mom would continually take back her dad after he cheated on her. That night while Daisy was lying in bed, she thought about her sister's comment and realized that there was some truth to what she said. Seeing her dad constantly moving in and out of the house affected Daisy. When she got older, she wondered why her father chose other women over his family. Why did he always leave? Weren't we enough? Then Daisy thought about her relationship with Ethan. Did she really love him, or did she just want him to choose her over all the other women? Did she want Ethan to do what her father failed to do?

We don't get to choose who our parents will be or what kind of upbringing we will have. Many children don't see a healthy relationship between their parents and that impacts the way that they view relationships. The emotional scars that we carry from childhood often resurface during adulthood. Look at your past relationships. What role did you play in why the relationship ended? Did you take responsibility for it? Were you healed from past hurts before you entered into a new relationship? If not, then you carry residue from your old situation into the new one. In Daisy's case, Ethan told her that he was going to see other women, and Daisy chose to stay and got hurt. She wanted Ethan to heal the hurt that her father had caused. But Ethan was the wrong person to heal her wounds. She wanted a person to choose her over others, instead of choosing to take her healing into her own hands like she needed to do. She wanted a man to choose her and rectify her past hurt. She wanted someone that she didn't need. She hoped he would correct something that she needed to correct for herself by not putting herself in hurtful situations. She needed to deal with her past to make better choices in her present.

> 3. You may say you want to know the truth but are unwilling to face/see the truth

Ashley met Eric at a bar and hit it off with him right away. He told her that he had been in a relationship for five years, and when it ended, it was really hard on him. He thought that he was going to marry his ex-girlfriend but found out that she had been cheating on him. After being hurt, he wasn't looking for a relationship; he just wanted to enjoy himself now that he was single. She really liked spending time with him and they started having sex regularly. After a while, Ashley wanted more than just casual sex; she wanted to be Eric's girlfriend. One night after they had slept together, as they were lying in bed, Ashley brought up the subject. "Eric, what do you think about us becoming exclusive, like boyfriend/girlfriend?" He took a deep breath and let out a big sigh. Eric got up out of bed and started to put on his clothes. "I told you from the beginning that I'm not ready for a relationship. I'm not ready to open myself up again and risk getting hurt. I thought I made myself clear." She laid there in the bed feeling more naked than she was. "But we spend a lot of time together and it just makes sense that we would give it a try, doesn't it?" she asked, hurt at how agitated he was getting. "Look, you knew what I was willing to give and I just don't want more than what we have. So if you want a boyfriend, then you're going to have to get someone else. If you can't handle what I can give, then we shouldn't see each other anymore." He was fully dressed and ready to leave. "I've got a busy day, so I'm going. You already know where I am with this. I told you from the beginning, and my feelings haven't changed. You want something that I can't give you, so it's probably time for the both of us to move on." And he was gone. Ashley thought about what he had said. She would rather be with him at any capacity than not be with him at all. She called his house knowing that he wasn't home and left a message on his machine. "Hey, I'm sorry for tonight. I've thought about it, and I'd like to go back to how we were. I understand that you're not ready for a committed relationship after being hurt. I hope that one day you will see that I won't hurt you. Call me."

Honesty is something that women say they want, but, even when the truth is right in front of them, they choose to manipulate it to be something they want to hear or see. Ashley was lying to both herself and Eric when she said that she wanted to go back to how they once were. She didn't want that type of relationship, but that was the only way she would still have Eric in her life. She was willing to give up what she really wanted in order to keep him on his terms. And that 'hope' that she has that one day he'll be ready to be in a relationship with her, that one day he'll realize that she wants to love him and not hurt him is a lie that she is telling herself. He never said, "Ashley one day I will be ready to be with you or love you." That is a fantasy/lie that she is telling herself to make it okay for her to change what she wants (a committed relationship) for what he will give her on his terms. Women often choose to either ignore the truth or make up a truth that is more appealing to them in order to reconcile within themselves what they are choosing to do.

    4. You're afraid to be lonely/alone

Many people are afraid to be alone or don't know how to be alone. It's easy to understand why. Look back on your life. Do you remember how old you were when you were in your very first relationship? How old were you when some boy smiled at you and you got all giggly? A lot of girls start dating at 13 and enjoy the beginning of a relationship and how a guy pays attention to her. He tells her she's pretty and she believes him. It sounds different coming from him than it does from her family. He validates her because she allows him to give her value. By the time she's 21, she's gone through different relationships that end, and she looks for the next one. She enjoys the early stages of a relationship enough that she tends to chronically date. Not a lot changes as you get older. There is the natural high that you get from flirting and having someone flirt with you. It's exciting and feels good.

After being in a relationship, women forget how to go to the movies or to restaurants by themselves. The younger a woman is when she starts dating, the more difficult it becomes to not date or be in a relationship.

What is it about relationships that makes a person desire them so much, to an unhealthy point? Let's look at this for a moment. You want someone to stay up all night talking to you on the phone. But, eventually, you need more to keep that high feeling, so you progress to the first kiss, which leads to a lot of kissing. That's enough for a while, then you're ready for more. Next comes petting/touching and then the ultimate, sex. Eventually, you fall into a routine with the person you are seeing, and things aren't as exciting as they once were. You don't talk on the phone all night, you're lucky if you get a call that's longer than half an hour. But you are in the cycle of kissing, touching and sex. But, after a while, it may become less and less romantic and more monotonous. At some point, it will become routine, and it takes more work and effort to be spontaneous and exciting. And really, unless you are married, men aren't going to put in very much work or effort.

So this is the cycle: you have someone to have sex, watch movies, eat meals, and just hang out with. But what if the person you are doing this with isn't a person you would want to marry? Why are you investing so much time with a person you can't see a future with? Why spend your time with a Mr. Right Now instead of just living your life until you meet your Mr. Right?

5. You may only be fulfilled in one area of a relationship and can't help but feel the void that you can't explain

So, when you are in a relationship where you do not feel fulfilled, the first thing to do is to identify what area you feel dissatisfied with. It's important to do this because identification of the issue is key to addressing it. If you try to make changes without first identifying the real issue, you risk making big changes and not feeling better because the problem still exists. Once you have identified what is bothering you, look at what role you play in creating or enabling the situation. Your action or lack of action may be a large part of the problem. It's important to examine yourself first because you can't change another person. The only person you can change is yourself. You will frustrate yourself to no end trying to make someone else change. So look at yourself and be honest about what steps you have taken to be in the situation you are in. Take responsibility for the choices you have made, and then look at the problem in the relationship. You must make the decision of whether you desire to try and work through the issues or if the problems are not worth keeping the relationship over if not then you may decide to end the relationship. If, however, you want to work through the issues, then you must approach your partner in a loving way and not in attack mode. He may not even be aware of how you are feeling. After you have spent time identifying the issue and thinking about the situation, you want to be careful not to bombard him. Remember, this is the first time he's learning about what you have been feeling, so be gentle and address the issue in a loving way. It is also important to note that you can't expect to get everything from one person. There may be areas that are better fulfilled by someone other than the person you are in a relationship with. If, for example, you enjoy volunteering and he doesn't, then you make time to volunteer while he spends time doing something he enjoys doing. You get your needs met and so does he, but you don't necessarily do it together.

> 6. That nagging feeling you have that something is off in your relationship = there is something off about your relationship

Alright, so, if you are in a relationship and you think that something is off, then that usually means that there is something off. Now, don't take action right away because it could be one of two things. The person in the relationship with you has either mentally or physically checked out.

There are times in a relationship when the man is evaluating his life, and he's not where he expected he would be. Mentally, he goes over the choices he has made or things that have happened, and how they have affected him. At these times, he mentally checks out and isn't very present in the relationship.

When a man checks out physically, is when he is no longer devoted to you. He is actively pursuing other women while still dealing with you. It's when you find out about him seeing other women that your relationship takes a new turn based on how you deal with it.

Again, it's important to know what you're dealing with before deciding to take action. Don't let your emotions take control of your actions because you may do something that you will later regret.

7. You ask men the wrong questions

Because women and men are so different, it shouldn't be surprising that we miss the mark more often than you'd think. So, when you want input from a man, first you must know that phrasing completely changes the kind of response you are looking for. Furthermore, what you hear isn't always what was said. To clarify, here are some examples of the wrong questions to ask.

- Do you love me?
- Do you want to be with me?
- Could you see yourself with me in the future?
- Do you want to get married someday?
- What are your goals for the future?

Instead of asking these questions, better questions to ask are:

- Are you in love with me? The reason this is a better way to ask the question is that a person can genuinely have feelings of love for or towards you. However, there is a big difference between feelings of love and being in love; and, if you do not make a clear distinction, you will be misleading yourself.

- What kind of relationship do you want to be in? This question is better to ask than asking [do you want to be with me, could you see yourself with me in the future, or do you want to get married someday?] These questions are too ambiguous; it leaves it so open into the near or far future that the questions don't really tell you what you really want to know. Instead, ask a question regarding the type of relationship he wants. If he doesn't know what kind of relationship he wants to be in, then he may not be ready to be in a relationship at all. You could also find out that the type of relationship he wants may not be the kind of relationship you want. Most men do want to be married someday, so asking if he wants to be married is different than if he wants to be married to you. Also, most men don't want to hurt a woman's feelings intentionally, so, when pressured, they may creatively answer the question. Don't forget to pay attention to his actions and his words.

- What is something you've accomplished in the past 6 months to a year that you are proud of? You want to know that he has set a goal and actually accomplished it. It's one thing to set goals, but it is very different to accomplish a goal. There are people that have many goals, but, if they aren't disciplined enough to take the steps to achieve what they desire, then they are dreamers more than doers.

8. You are either oblivious to your category or in denial of it

Knowing that men categorize all women, the next thing to discover is how you are categorized. The best thing about knowing that men categorize women is that you control your category by how you choose to talk, dress, and take action. Now that you know those are the things men watch for, think about what roles you have been. Have you been a 3rd, 2nd, or Main? If you are still unsure, look back at the qualities of each role to see which you have been and know that you control how you are categorized.

From Price Tag To Priceless

Chapter Six – The Girl Program

When it comes to relationships, the tools girls are given differ from the ones given to boys. This diversification of tools starts from the time the parents know the baby's sex. We have different colors, toys/games, and clothes. We're programmed differently, and, when dealing with relationships, we wonder why we misunderstand each other.

It's a Girl:

When this announcement is made, what usually happens is that there is a mad rush to go out and pastel-ize the new nursery. I would say that there is a pink explosion, but that isn't as true nowadays. You may have a combination of pinks/light purples, anything pastel. Go through the baby section of stores and there really is no way to not know what items are intended for girls. Take a look at the kinds of pictures on the girls' baby clothes - you will see an array of flower prints, poka dots, rainbow stripes, and cute little animals like butterflies or ladybugs.

In general, the honorary color for a girl is pink. But why? Why pink and not another color; possibly because of the preconceived ideas or associations to the color pink. And what does pink say? Pink says: soft, pleasant, innocent, pure, pretty. But why isn't red the "little girl" color? Perhaps it's because it carries a different color connotation. Red says: bold, loud, look at me, racy. Red is more "woman" than "little girl". Therefore, pink is the color to wrap your newborn innocent baby girl in. After you have walked through the infant clothing area in the store, take a stroll over to the toddler section and then make your way to the girls section and pay attention to how much pink you see. It will be plenty of pink, but you will start to see a lot more color combinations and options.

Something I have to mention which is more of a sidebar but you will notice if you do go and look at clothing for girls: there is a drastic contrast in styles. You will have some girls clothing that looks very innocent and child-like and then you will see some clothing that seems like it was for a young adult or juniors section style of clothing shrunk down to little girls' sizes. I mention it because it's one of those things that makes fathers cringe to pass by the little girls section and see mini-skirts, see-through material, two-piece outfits, and extremely short shorts. But it is important to pay attention to why the fathers react in this way, the "cringe".

Happily Ever After:

After the pink period comes the happily ever after phase. From the time we are little girls, we learn about happily ever after. We have books with stories about how a beautiful girl or in some cases a princess, who is innocent, kind, well-liked, and beautiful falls into a problematic situation. This situation usually isn't her fault. Many times the problem is jealousy or greed, but the important thing is that the beautiful girl is not at fault for the drama in the story. Even though she is not at fault, she's always the one to suffer because of the problem. And she always bears the problem(s), not complaining, but her kind nature shines through dealing with it and making the best of the situation.

The beautiful girl is then given some companions in the story to help her through the situation, whether they are other people or animals. Through their friendship you get to see how good and well-liked she is, demonstrating her good character.

Then the story climaxes when she is faced with danger and her champion appears and saves her. Throughout the story you hear a little bit about the champion, how he too is good looking and of good character. He has seen the beautiful girl on some chance meeting, and if there is an interaction between them it is usually brief, but that is all it takes for him to know that she is the one for him. Throughout the story, you hear about how he has been searching for the beautiful girl, and he always finds her in time to save her. He saves her and then proclaims his love for her and they get married and live happily ever after. After hearing these stories, we desire to be that beautiful girl, who, in most cases, is or becomes a princess.

So, from birth we have learned to be "pink". To be pure and innocent and then, from the stories read to us, we learn that our reward for being "pink" is that a handsome prince-like person will come into our lives and rescue us. He will tell us that he loves us and ask us to marry him and we will live happily ever after. Ok, now what?

Playing House:

Well, now it's time to learn about the post-marriage ceremony. So we get a baby doll, fake food and tea dish set, and also our own kid-size broom and other cleaning products. The interesting thing about this is that we go from "pink" to happily ever after then we skip the 'honeymoon' and go straight to the baby doll. No one tells us how the baby doll arrives; we just know that it is here and we are to take care of it, learn how to cook and set the table, and keep a clean house. On this program, which lasts from birth to about 4 years old, we learn to: be good girls, fall for the handsome prince (who has already fallen for us), take care of our baby doll and of our household. Now that we have the big picture taken care of, it's time to learn a new lesson.

How to keep your man:

For this lesson we get introduced to a new toy – Barbie. She teaches us many lessons. First, she is beautiful. She has beautiful hair, the perfect body, perfect feet for high heels; her make-up is done just right, and the perfect smile. In addition to her perfect outward appearance, she comes with her "how to keep a man" toolkit - accessories. She has a lot of clothes, purses, shoes, sun glasses, earrings, and jewelry in general. She has everything she needs to make herself visually appealing and can diversify her look with a new costume. In addition to her look; she also has a pet, or at times siblings to watch over, and a group of faithful, beautiful friends. It's important to note that her friends are loyal to her and would never try and take Ken's attention away from Barbie. And she also has an array of vehicles, mobile homes, and homes that she owns. She can also have any type of career she wants. She is an independent beautiful woman and with as many assets as she has, what man in his right mind would ever leave her? None! Not even when he could choose from any of her friends because he is the only guy. Nope, he stays with Barbie. She is the only one that has everything from accessories, to vehicles, to multiple homes. Barbie teaches girls what we have to have to make ourselves desirable. By keeping our independence and staying attractive, we can keep our man.

New Environment - Adaptability:

Up to this point, girls have been on the pink-princess-mommy-Barbie track, and parents have done their best to guide their girls in a particular way, and then it's time for school. Once school starts, girls are introduced to classmates from different backgrounds, and not all girls have been on the same program track as they have. With the introduction of new friends from different upbringings comes the integration of new games and ideas. Now, in the classroom girls, are provided with an opportunity to play house in a different capacity than when they were at home. In the safety of their home, playing house consisted of a little girl, her baby doll, and maybe a stuffed animal playing her pretend husband. Now that she is in school, a real boy gets to be her pretend husband.

At home, the stuffed animal did everything she told him and there was no conflict because she controlled the situation. At school with a real boy playing her husband, he has his own ideas of how his household should be run and conflict arises. In this setting, if she doesn't do what her pretend husband wants, he has the option to replace her with another girl who is willing to do what he wants.

How does she reconcile this conflict? Up to this point, she has been in charge. She controlled her dolls, toys, her imagination, and made up the game. Now she has something to lose.

- She can be replaced with another female classmate
- She learns that if she does something unpopular, she can run the risk of sitting alone at lunch
- She can become a target for teasing
- She can be ignored

A new set of problematic situations are introduced with this new change of environment. After seeing and possibly experiencing some of the above consequences, she learns that she has a choice in how she is treated. She can be herself and run the risk of facing a consequence, or she can compromise. Most people would rather be liked than not liked, and, faced with this situation, many girls choose to compromise.

To Change Or Not To Change:

Deciding whether to be an individual or a carbon copy, is a decision we make early in life. On one hand, our parents tell us we are special and unique, and to be ourselves. On the other hand, if being ourselves at school makes us a target for being ostracized and cast out, it becomes harder to want to be ourselves.

We all desire love and want to belong, but what if the price for being included means not being true to you? As an adult, you have a different freedom than when you're a child. As an adult, you can search out a group you fit with. You can go online and find like-minded people. You can move from a small town to a large, diverse city. You can choose what neighborhood to live in. But as a child, you don't have the ability to change your environment. Many children adapt to survive in the environment they are in. At times, that survival means sacrificing who you really are to be accepted.

Once a child learns how to change themselves to be accepted, making compromises becomes easier. Then what becomes difficult is really knowing who you are. Fitting into a group, can come with the price of losing yourself.

As young girls get older, the opportunities for them to choose to blend into the crowd or be themselves continue. Girls who have been sheltered, told positive things about themselves, and are given an abundance of love are taught how to love. These girls have a better chance at being themselves because they have been taught by those who love them that the most important thing to be is themselves. They are beautiful just the way they are, and they are loveable. As they grow older, because they have had more positive examples of love, they have a better chance at recognizing the real from counterfeit.

Girls who have had to face difficult life circumstances like violence, abuse (of any kind), or have been told negative things about themselves have a more difficult time finding real love. The lessons they may have learned in life due to what they have been exposed to or experienced may make it hard for them to really love themselves. After hearing negative things and being mistreated, it is difficult to love themselves, and they begin to try to please others and learn to compromise to receive what they think is love. You want to believe that you are loveable and desire for someone to love you. Women that have this deficiency of self-worth and self-love, sadly, are easy for men to spot.

Men teach boys a different program and this lesson-how to spot an easy prey-is sadly part of the training for many males. Unfortunately, many times women that have low self-esteem directly tell men that they don't love/like themselves. These women are looking for validation, which in many cases they will receive, but after a quick fix, the feeling doesn't last long, and she continues to seek someone to fill that void.

Growing from childhood to adulthood, you may not have had much of a choice in what you were exposed to. But as adults, you do have many choices on what kind of impact those experiences have in your present and future. For some people, the negative things that they have been raised to think about themselves are very difficult to change. But they can be changed.

As an adult, you can choose:
- who to allow in your life
- whether to get counseling to help work through your past
- what types of coping mechanisms to use
- how to learn to love yourself
- to believe that you are lovable and deserve love

Whether or not a girl was brought up with the Girl Program described above, all girls have encountered situations that provided them with the opportunity to compromise themselves. While it is appealing to belong to the group, it comes with a heavy price. The cost of belonging is one that you may not see or understand until later in life when you ask questions like 'how did I even get here', 'when did I stop being me', or 'what would make me happy?'

Think back on past relationships you have been in. Can you recognize moments that you compromised and it wasn't worth it? You may have lost a lot over the years. But the great thing is that you can stop, step back/look back, identify choices you made that weren't the best for you, and make a decision to change. And deciding to make a change doesn't mean that you don't ever compromise; it means that the compromises you choose to make are ones that strengthen your relationship and, at the same time, won't cause you harm. In the following examples, you will see an unhealthy and healthy compromise to better understand.

***

Vivian and Danny had been dating for two months when he told her that he was having a difficult time being monogamous. He was used to casually dating/having sex with women, but this was the first time he had committed to being a boyfriend, and he was finding it difficult. Vivian really liked Danny and didn't want the relationship to end. She asked him what she could do to help him deal with the struggles of being in a committed relationship for the first time. Then he said what she didn't want to hear "well I just don't think it's fair to you and I don't want to hurt you so I think we should break-up." Vivian didn't want to lose him; she felt strong feelings for him and loved being with him. "Listen Vivian, I really like being with you, but it has been really hard for me to be with just you. I thought I was ready to be in a committed relationship, but I guess I'm not. You are an amazing person, but I like you too much to hurt you, and I'd rather be upfront with you than mess up and hurt you later." They broke-up and went their separate ways. It was not long before they ran into each other while they were out and started talking again. After hanging out, they ended up sleeping together with 'no strings attached' and fell into a regular routine of hanging out and then having sex. Danny was the only man she was seeing, while Danny was seeing several women and still seeing Vivian. She didn't like that he was seeing other women. He told her that she was different, and she thought eventually he would realize that she was the one he really wanted to be with. Then Vivian got the bad news. She went for her annual check-up and the results showed that she had contracted an STD. She knew she had contracted the STD from Danny because he was the only person she had sex with since her last check-up. She was devastated!

***

Simon and Tessa had been dating for two months and it was great! They spent all their free time together. They went to work and would call each other on their lunch break. Then after work, they would go out to eat and spend hours together until he dropped her off at her house and called her on his way back home, and they would stay on the phone all night. Then one day Simon said "Tessa we've got to talk." She looked at him and began to worry about what he was going to say. "I love spending time with you and talking to you but it's really affecting me. I'm not getting anything done around my house, and it's hard for me to get up for work after talking all night on the phone. I'm struggling to get through the work day because I'm so tired." She nodded her head, understanding what he was saying because she was also having a hard time getting through her workday. "So I think I have to be better at managing my time. I still love spending time with you, but I have to do it in a smarter way." Tessa knew that what Simon was saying made sense for both of them, but she was afraid of what 'managing' his time better would mean for their relationship. Although she was concerned about how making changes would affect their relationship, she was willing to make adjustments and support the changes he needed to make. So the next day Simon went to work and texted her a cute message while he was on his lunch break. Then after work he went home and cleaned up his apartment and called Tessa to invite her over for dinner. She came over and enjoyed the first home cooked meal Simon had made for them and was impressed by his cooking skills. After dinner they talked while washing the dishes together. Then they watched one of his favorite shows. After the show was over it was 11 p.m. and he got up from the couch and thanked Tessa for coming over. "Would you like to come over to my place tomorrow for dinner?" she asked. He answered, "well I have plans to watch the game with the guys tomorrow but how about the day after that?" She agreed and spent the next night catching up with her girlfriends, whom she had neglected since dating Simon. Eventually they fell into a routine of seeing each other every other day and spending most of the weekend together. At first Tessa was afraid that spending less time together would affect their relationship but it ended up making their relationship better. She realized that she didn't have to be with him all the time and he always made the effort to text her funny cute messages on the days they didn't spend together. With spending time apart, their relationship got better.

When you are secure in who you are and what you have to offer, making compromises in a relationship isn't threatening. Know what you are willing to negotiate on and what is non-negotiable and stick to them. Don't make compromises that cause you harm or affect your self-worth doing so results in losing yourself.

Not all girls started out on the same program, but it doesn't mean that all women can't have their happy ending. Instead of being in a problematic situation and waiting for your prince to come in and rescue you, think about how *you* can better your situation. Why star in a story where you have to be rescued or where you and he rescue each other? Wouldn't it be better for you to be in a good place within yourself? First, work on becoming a complete and whole person before desiring to be in a relationship. Find out who you really are and what you value. Once you are complete, you can tell real love from counterfeit. A person that is complete doesn't settle for a 'quick fix' that leaves you more depleted than before he came into your life.

From Price Tag To Priceless

Chapter Seven – Boys Play Games, Girls Play Pretend

Looking back on the types of toys my brother had verses the type of toys I had is a clue about how differently boys and girls are raised. I played with baby dolls, with plastic food and a tea set, played dress up, while he played games like checkers, battle ship, and with a football. He busied himself with games while I played pretend.

He learned things like rules, strategy, short cuts, scoring, and winning. I learned how to make things look nice, how to take care of things, and how to make everything have a happily ever after. No wonder we make a mess of relationships! From the beginning we are programmed for miscommunication.

As we get older, not a lot changes. Men still play games and women still pretend. Let's look at the games men play (i.e. character roles) so that women can at least recognize the game and learn some of the characteristics.

Mr. Blamer

He usually has a sob story about how he's in a situation where he really should be further in life than he actually is, and the reason he doesn't have it all together is the result of how life has cheated him. He's the victim of everything. Some examples of life cheating him are as follows:

- Didn't have a father around to teach him to be a man
- Teachers didn't like him and gave him a hard time
- Baby-Mama-Drama > a crazy ex-girlfriend who he unexpectedly had a child with who tries to take everything he has including his time with their child
- Bosses never like him so it's hard to keep a job

Mr. Blamer is easy to identify because he has an excuse for everything. He rarely takes any responsibility over his role in the situation.

Mr. Wounded Sparrow

His story is about how his relationship recently ended and how he is badly hurt. He is traumatized by the break up and can't bring himself to enter into a monogamous/committed relationship for fear of being hurt again. However, he is definitely looking for "fun" and keeping it light, so he is into casual sex. But can't bring himself to be vulnerable enough to put himself in a situation where he might get hurt. So his heart is closed because he needs time to heal while his genitals are open for business.

Mr. Dreamy/Mr. Nightmare

He tells you the things you've always wanted to hear. He suggests moving the relationship to the next level before you even thought about it. He sets the tone in the relationship like wanting to be exclusive fairly soon after meeting. He talks about moving in together and makes future plans with you and tells you how your lives would be if you were married. He may even talk to you about having kids with him. Then he suddenly changes, and he's not the same person. He becomes distant, and when the two of you are together he's not really present. He seems easily agitated and cold. In the beginning, he was going 100mph, and now he's going 5mph. He wants more space and talks about how things are moving too fast. (Remember he set the pace to begin with.) Then he either breaks up with you or pulls a disappearing act and doesn't call/return calls.

Mr. Knight In Shining Armor (for a price)

He makes himself available to rescue you whenever you need him. He says things like, "if you go out and drink too much, don't try and drive home. Just call me, and I'll pick you up." He always puts himself in the position to be your helper and builds you up emotionally by paying you compliments. But he does have a motive! In case the situation presents itself, he is ready and willing to be there for you sexually.

Mr. Player

Plays the field and that's all he wants to do. He is usually 21-30 years old. The player not only plays the game, he really believes in the game. He lives his life by the rules of the game. He will pass up the "Main and 2nd" girls to play with the 3rds. He not only believes in the game, he also teaches the game to other men. He ridicules the men that are committed to one woman.

Mr. Honest

He tells women straight up what he is about. If he just wants to have sex with a woman, he tells her. Some women won't stand for it, while other women will agree to be with him on his terms, thinking that they are two consenting adults doing what they want to do in the here and now. Most times those women find themselves developing feelings for the man and get hurt when they want more and he reminds them of what he wanted in the beginning, which hasn't changed for him. Mr. Honest is telling you the truth – believe him. "I'm not looking to be in a relationship right now." When you hear something like that, leave him alone.

Mr. Nice

He is too nice to your friends and family. He does this for his benefit, not yours. Just in case the two of you don't work out he has other options in your circle of friends/family. They have only seen him on his good behavior and they explain the fact that the two of you not working out as merely that you weren't meant to be together. He groomed himself to have your friends/family like him so much that they can explain away the awkwardness of your relationship not working out and it being alright for him to pursue someone else in your circle.

Mr. Sensitive

He opens up and shares with you. He's also sympathetic to you and what you are going through. He uses being sensitive to be vulnerable in front of you. Because of his strategy, you think that this makes you and your relationship special. Often times, he has had a road map to women because he was raised in a single parent home with his mother. He understands women in a different way because of his inside track; and when he decides to abuse it, he causes a lot of heartache.

Mr. Rebel

Usually called the bad boy who is always attractive in theory, but, as you get to know him more, you learn that he is usually very aimless. He has things he complains about but rarely ever wants to put in the effort to make a change. He has opinions that he quotes, but when confronted about what role he will play to make things better, he's not really interested.

Mr. Intellect

He can be very appealing because he draws you in with his knowledge and opinions. He enjoys debates; it's sort of foreplay for him. He takes pleasure in the challenge of making you see things from his perspective, and his ultimate goal is to get you to eventually agree that what he says is right.

Mr. Apprentice

He is being coached by either older men or by his friends, and dating him can be very confusing. He is a bit schizophrenic because at times he behaves in one way and at other times his behavior is completely different. Often times when you date "Mr. Apprentice," you find yourself replaying your encounters with him and something is always off, but you're not quite sure what that is. But it's him. He is off. He does not know who he wants to be, which ends up confusing both him and you.

Mr. Relentless

He is fun to watch in social settings. You can spot him by his behavior of mingling with all the girls. He will win over a girl by sheer law of averages. He will walk up to a group of girls and ask all of them one by one to dance. When one woman says 'no', he moves right on to the next the girl. He doesn't ever seem to be discouraged by women continually turning him down because, eventually, one will say 'yes'.

Mr. Comedian

He's pretty self-explanatory. The clown, he will do whatever it takes to make you laugh. His game usually always works because who doesn't like to laugh? The problem with him is that he doesn't know when to be serious, or you don't take him seriously. Once you date him, you may find that he is actually very insecure with a people-pleasing type of personality.

Mr. Cool

He usually has a quality about how he carries himself that he doesn't have to do very much work to attract a woman. Usually it's the women that throw themselves at him. They make themselves available to him in whatever capacity he will take them.

Mr. Pitiful

He usually has a very sad story to tell about how his life is gone, and the saddest part is that it's true. Women tend to have 'pity sex' with him because they feel for him. In a group of men, he is easy to pick out because he is usually socially awkward and just doesn't look happy. In social settings, his conversation is inappropriate in that he talks about 'heavy' or depressing things that he's gone through, and women genuinely feel badly for him.

Mr. Church Player

This man causes so much damage to women. He attracts women by how he conducts himself. But the thing to remember is that if he is really right within his spiritual walk then he wouldn't put you in a compromising position. He would not ask you or lead you to do things that would make you feel uncomfortable.

Mr. Best Friend

He can cause a lot of damage as well because he has invested time getting to know you, which makes you very vulnerable to him. The thing is that women tend to be very relational. Women enjoy sharing and giving, which can be very problematic if they don't use wisdom. You share too much information with him, and, when the time comes, he'll use it. Because he knows you so well, he knows what to say to encourage or discourage you. One way to know that you are dealing with a "Mr. Best Friend" is that if you are dating someone, he chimes in and plants comments like, "you're such a great person and you deserve to be treated so much better than he treats you." Or "if I had someone like you, I wouldn't treat you the way he does." In other words, he tends to say things that from one angle may sound like a compliment to you, but, from another angle, he's planting thoughts in your mind that would in some way benefit him.

Mr. Opportunist

The opportunist does just that. He uses friendship as a strategy to study the women he is interested in. He makes himself available to learn about her past, and she always opens up and says too much. He just waits until she gives him the signal that he's been waiting for. An example of a signal she will give is to say something like "I'm just so lonely, and lately I've been feeling really vulnerable." He's heard her signal, and he makes his move.

***

The most important thing to remember is that when a man is not wanting/ready to be in a committed relationship and is playing the field, he won't only run one play. So a man that is playing the field will be a combination of the "Mr.'s" listed above. Men are strategists, and, if they ran the same play continuously, their strategy would be found out and they would lose.

So here is the kicker: more than likely, the man you end up with is a reformed man who used to be one of the

"Mr.'s" mentioned above. Unfortunately, the game plays get passed down from man to man, and it takes them wanting to have something real and different for them to change. (They have to make the change for themselves, not for you!) It is your responsibility to decide what you want in a relationship, figure out what your standards are, and stick to them. Don't settle for what a man chooses to offer. Know what kind of treatment you want, and, if a man offers you less, walk away. He might be the right guy, but it may not be the right time. Walking away, you don't loss anything. The right man will not want you to be compromised, not even by him. He will respect the fact that you respect and value yourself.

Boys were taught strategy and girls played pretend. Stop pretending; wake-up and see things as they really are instead of how you would like them to be. Think back to men from your past. Can you really see them now? In the future, really watch how men approach women, and pay attention to what they say when they talk to you. If you hear what you want to hear instead of what is really said, you're still pretending. And the only person you hurt by pretending is you.

The Roles	Description	Game Plays (3 additional roles he uses)
Mr. Blamer	has a sob story, nothing is his fault, things happen to him, has an excuse for everything	Wounded Sparrow Dreamy/Nightmare Sensitive
Mr. Wounded Sparrow	hurt from last relationship so isn't ready to be in a committed relationship	Blamer Honest Sensitive
Mr. Dreamy/ Mr. Nightmare	says all the right things to move the relationship to the next level then switches on you and becomes distant	Church Player Sensitive Wounded Sparrow
Mr. Knight In Shining Armor	puts himself in the position to be your helper and builds you up emotionally	Best Friend Opportunist Honest
Mr. Player	believes in the game, lives by the rules of the game, and teaches the game to others	Cool Intellect Nice
Mr. Honest	says what he wants or doesn't want from the beginning and when she wants more he reminds her what he said in the beginning	Comedian Intellect Best Friend

Mr. Nice	Nice (in public) just in case things don't work, he has more options with people you know	Sensitive Honest Intelligent
Mr. Sensitive	he opens up and tells you a lot, you do the same and he has the inside track on how to manipulate you emotionally	Wounded Sparrow Best Friend Dreamy/Nightmare
Mr. Rebel	has an opinion about everything but takes no action on how to fix things he rebels/complains about	Cool Intellect Honest
Mr. Intellect	draws you in with knowledge and opinions; likes to debate	Honest Cool Opportunist
Mr. Relentless	keeps asking girls out until one says yes (may keep asking the same girls out as well)	Pitiful Opportunist Apprentice
Mr. Apprentice	coached by others on the game and also his own opinions mixed in so he's confused which confuses you as well	Sensitive Nice Best Friend
Mr. Comedian	does what it takes to make you laugh, hard to take him serious, caution: may have a very dark/depressing side to him	Intellect Cool Rebel

Mr. Cool	attracting women is effortless for him, caution: he doesn't know how to work at relationships	Rebel Intellect Honest
Mr. Pitiful	his sad story draws sympathy from women	Blamer Honest Wounded Sparrow
Mr. Church Player	seems the right kind of guy but because he influences you to alter your standards or compromise yourself	Intellect Best Friend Honest
Mr. Best Friend	he has the inside track on you so can influence you when convenient	Sensitive Honest Opportunist
Mr. Opportunist	is close to you so when the opportunity presents itself he is ready	Best Friend Knight in Shining Armor Cool

The Roles	Description
Mr. Right	Many times he is a reformed "Mr." He is tired of playing games and is ready to be with one woman. He becomes ready on his terms. It won't take a good or the right woman to make him change. He changes when he is ready. He may remember a woman that he hurt in the past that left him because of his game playing or he may look for a new woman to be the one he wants to settle down with. The way you can identify him from the others is that he doesn't want you or your standards/values compromised. He is willing to wait for you and he isn't seeing any one else while he is waiting. He wants to be committed to you. He cares about your reputation and won't taint it. He introduces you to his friends and family and wants you with him when he spends time with them at gatherings and family functions. He meets your family and considers the fact that they may become his family if he marries you. He is invested because he wants to be not because he has to be (to get what he wants). He sees your value and thus treats you as if you are valuable to him.

* The 3 additional roles or game plays listed are the most common ones he may use, but he is not limited to three or four roles. He can use as many as he likes to attract and keep a woman at arms' length, ready for his phone call and at his disposal.

From Price Tag To Priceless

Chapter Eight – Fooled By A Feeling

What if every time you got a craving to eat something unhealthy, you did it? You would not only listen to that craving, but you would go to a buffet so that you could eat as much as you possibly could. Initially, you would get a stomach ache and all you would want to do afterwards is go to sleep. A long-term consequence of doing this over a period of time is that your clothes would probably not fit as well as they used to. More than likely, you would get a craving for something and go right back into getting it satisfied and repeat the cycle.

Well, running out and taking action based on feelings is very similar. Feelings are fickle and more value is placed on them than should be. You meet a man and *feel* a connection and make a decision to become invested. Levels of involvement vary. Once you have a feeling about a person, you start to do a combination of things like romanticize, plan, and take action to deepen the level of involvement.

Some women meet a man, have a feeling about him, and take immediate action by asking for some sort of contact information or actually set up a date to investigate this feeling she has. Other women take a different, more passive approach. The tactic used may be more of an internal process which includes romanticizing the situation and thinking out what might happen between the two of them. Using this method, women become quite creative in trying to plan a spontaneous way for them to meet again. This planned "spontaneous" meeting will, of course, include elements like her looking perfect in the outfit that accentuates all of her assets, her hair and make-up being perfect-basically her looking flawless! Taking this method also involves her thinking out how the conversation between them would go, so that when this meeting takes place, she has the right sort of responses to his comments that are a combination of wit and flirtation.

So let's say that whichever tactic is used, be it direct or indirect, you have your second meeting with the man, and now the stakes have risen. Now that your involvement with the man is no longer one-sided, the game really begins, and we can take a deeper look at where the 'feeling' can lead you.

Now that you have made first contact and are on track to follow this feeling path, the level of investment and involvement becomes deeper. You start to think of ways to bring him up in conversations with your friends. You think of funny things to tell him the next time he calls. Eventually you encompass him in your daily routine. You think of him when he isn't around. You listen intently when he speaks to hear his likes and dislikes, and you begin to incorporate or eliminate things accordingly. You plan around him. And when his actions fall short of your expectations you make excuses for the shortcomings, searching for reasons why he did not say or do what you wanted/expected/or wished he would do or say. All of this energy is because of a feeling.

You invested so much without much of an effort on his part. The problem is that the feelings begin a trickle effect from your emotions to your mind, which leads you to taking action. It's kind of scary how quickly this can happen. Those that may be in bit of denial, think about a time you had a crush on someone. Well, that crush started with a feeling. You may or may not have taken physical action based on the feelings you felt, but, either way, you did invest some time in thinking about a person based on the feelings you had.

So are we all on the same page? We have all felt this feeling whether it stayed in the 'crush box' category, where no further action was taken by you, or it became something you decided to take some kind of action towards. We all can admit that we know this 'feeling'.

Alright, so now that we have identified this feeling and its process, we can dive into where this can lead. So the feeling has been felt, and now has to meet and contend with the romantic image that the woman has developed in her mind of her Mr. Right. Usually, the Mr. Right has been so romanticized and built up that no person can realistically measure up to the imaginary idea. And where do women find their basis for material to compare the man they've met to the Mr. Right in their mind? Movies, books, songs, and stories of other relationships they have heard about. The key is that if you take characteristics from a combination of men real and mythological, you can construct your idea of the perfect man but realistically you won't find him.

After spending time with the man that you've met, you start to see the ways that the man before you doesn't do or say the things you've wanted the man of your dreams to. And at this point, some women end the relationship because he is not living up to the image in her mind. Other women are intrigued by the feelings they have for the man and decide to investigate this romantic situation. Now I must clearly state that there is nothing wrong with wanting to investigate an interest you may have for another unmarried person. However, the time investment in a relationship becomes problematic when you ultimately attempt to ignore or deny that the relationship you have willingly put yourself in is unhealthy.

When dealing with relationships, don't just follow a feeling; look at the facts. Is the man that you are interested in available? Is he employed? Does he want to be in a committed relationship? You have to look at elements other than feelings so that you are not blinded by them. The difficult thing to come to terms with is that it is not the men that have fooled the women. Instead, women act foolishly and end up hurt. I know that this sounds harsh, but women must take responsibility for the roles they play in relationships. When you set standards and live by them, you can look at a man, and, if he doesn't meet those crucial standards, then walk away. Why spend time with someone you know that you wouldn't want to spend the rest of your life with? If you want to be married, stop investing time in men that you know you don't or won't want to spend a lifetime with. Remember, just because something *feels* good doesn't mean that it is good *for* you.

From Price Tag To Priceless

Chapter Nine – Courtship VS. Dating

As time passes, how we do things changes, and one of these changes is language. Certain words are lost, with progression, and new words are created to define or describe the days we currently live in. Courtship, for instance, is a word that is not used as frequently as it used to be. Today, people use the word 'dating' instead. But the words do not mean the same thing, and the word 'dating' doesn't hold a universal value. By not having a universal value, the use of a word that is defined differently can cause a lot of confusion and hurt.

First, let's look at the word 'courtship'. Courtship is comprised of two individual words 'court' and 'ship'. When used as a verb, court means: to try to win the favor of, to seek affections of; to attempt to gain; to invite. The favorable outcome of courting is marriage. Now, when the word court is used as a noun, court is a place where justice is administered or upheld. There is a hearing, and either a judge and/or jury determines the outcome of the cases.

Now, the second part of courtship is the word 'ship'. Ship means: to cause to be transported by or a vessel for transportation. Initially, looking at the word 'ship' as it pertains to 'love' may not make much sense, but if we probe deeper into the kinds of phrases used when talking about love, we can see a correlation. For instance, many of the phrases used when talking about love are often the following: 'fall in love', 'fallen in love', 'fell in love', 'falling in love', and 'being in love.' All of the statements read as though a person was in one state but, as a result of 'love', have now been moved or *shipped* into a different state. So, a person was in one state or category but, after encountering love, has moved into another category. They go from an 'I' to a 'we'. When making plans, they now have to check with their partner before committing.

With the word 'courtship' being defined a little better, now we can look at the word 'date/dating'. Date can be defined as a commitment to go out socially with another person, usually because of romantic interest.

It is now more common to use the word 'date,' but with different generations, other words are used like 'talking/ talking to' and 'seeing'. So, with the different words that are available to use, why use one over another? Well, there is more intent or purpose for using specific words than you would think.

The word 'courtship' was used in the past because a man used the word in order to attain a wife. He wanted to be married. But in order to become married, he had to demonstrate that he was capable of taking care of a wife. The parents of the woman he was interested in would examine the man's situation and, in a sense, they 'took him to court' to see if he was worthy of taking their daughter as his wife. And I use the word 'taking' in reference to the vows spoken, "do you take this…to be your lawful…" By 'taking him to court,' the parents of the woman examined the man's situation. They took the following kinds of questions into consideration before allowing a man to court their daughter:

- Did the man approach the parents before approaching their daughter?
- Does this man have a job > means to take care of their daughter?
- Does this man have a home > a place to take their daughter to live?
- What is this man's credit > does he have good credit or bad credit (if bad then why?)
- How does this man take care of himself and his belongings (what kind of attention does he put into presenting himself?)
- What kind of a family does this man come from (do they have a good reputation?)
- Does this man attend church/believe in God?
- What kind of reputation does the man have?
- Does this man keep his word/is he trustworthy?

- What has he accomplished?

- What is the longest amount of time the man has worked at a job (does he have the discipline to work a job?)

- Is he a responsible man?

The parents took all of these things into consideration before allowing him to approach their daughter. By going through this process, the parents had a full view of the case or the man's situation. They knew what type of man they're entrusting with their daughter. The parents knew whether or not the match or relationship would be a favorable situation for their daughter. Now, the questions above didn't ask anything pertaining to 'love', but there is a reason for it. If a man can take care of himself and take special care of his belongings, then there is a greater possibility that, if entrusted with their daughter, he would also take special care of her. He demonstrated the ability to be responsible and invested time in taking care of or placed care in the things he deemed important. Now, if you cringe at the word 'thing' as if you are an item to be owned, remember the kind of language used when talking about love, phrases like: 'we are one', 'we belong to each other', 'he/she's with me', 'two halves of one whole', and of course in marriage vows 'do you take this man/woman to have and to hold...'

The process of courtship allowed parents to examine a young man's situation and then determine whether or not he would be allowed to become acquainted with their daughter under their supervision. By providing supervision, the parents were able to set the types of interactions they felt were appropriate for a young man to get to know their daughter and still maintain her virtue, which was guarded for her future husband. By deciding to court a young woman, a man knew that he was making a commitment to get to know a woman before deciding to marry her. He wanted to know what she thought about different topics, what her temperament was, what kind of character she had, and what her goals/dreams were to see if they lined up with his. The young man and woman made a commitment to get to know each other by engaging in a courtship. During their courtship they had supervised or chaperoned visits. Often their physical contact or touching was very limited. Why? Well, when you cross the barriers of touching and becoming intimate, it is difficult to think clearly. After touching, all kinds of senses are awakened and can be very misleading. Instead of staying in the logical and analytical state, a flood of emotions rush in. Phrases like 'butterflies in my stomach', 'walking on air' and 'gives me goose bumps' have been used to explain this new found feeling. Now you are led by what you 'feel' and not by what you 'know,' which is dangerous territory, an area that cannot be trusted! This is the: WARNING, WARNING, DANGER place! While in the courtship stage, parents prevented entering this zone. By not entering into this danger zone, you are then able to make better choices for yourself based on facts versus feelings.

    Dating, however, is very different. Now-a-days, most people choose to date/talk instead of courting. The way dating works is a man will see a woman that 'catches his eye,' and he will approach her and talk to her. He finds out her name, phone number and where she lives. He talks with her and learns about her. He learns things like where she went to school and where she works. Their "getting to know" each other conversation, is fairly general information, and they set a date. They meet or he might pick her up and drive to a location where they are entertained by watching a movie, play, do an activity, or go have a meal together. During this date, their conversation seems to be a bit general with some personal facts thrown into the conversation to allow the other person to begin to get to know some of their likes/dislikes. At the end of the date, there may/may not be an embrace and/or kiss. Second date goes very similarly to the first date and so on. After a few or maybe after several dates, the level of intimate exchanges increases, and there is less and less personal space between them. At some point, the woman will bring the man to introduce him to her family and friends. By this time, she is already so invested in him and in her relationship with him that if her friends/family raise any concerns about the man, she doesn't listen to them and instead is quick to defend him. She defends him because, according to her, 'they don't know him like she knows him'. She has several reasons for why she sees a different side of him than her friends/family, and they aren't giving him a chance. Her bond with him becomes stronger, and if her friends and family (who, by the way, have loved and known her longer than this new man) continues to give him a hard time, then an 'it's us against the world' mentality comes into play. Now, not only is she in the relationship with him, but there is a forbidden element to the relationship which makes it more appealing to her, a sort of romantic notion that she blindly embraces.

By the time the woman introduces the man to her friends and family, she has already made up her mind that she is invested in the relationship and is ready to defend it. She decides that her family and friends, who know and love her, *don't* really know and love her. Why the change? And why is she so defensive? Well, one reason is that they are questioning her choice in a potential mate. They question the person she presents as the one she is trusting with her heart, and this hurts her. She is quick to defend the man because she is defensive about the fact that they are essentially questioning her. If the family/friends don't believe that the man she presents to them is worthy of having her, then she is defensive that they are questioning her ability to see the man clearly for who and what he really is. A part of the defensive position she takes is defending her own judgment, but, by this time, she has already been intimate with the man, and she is much more invested. She has 'fallen in love' and is no longer seeing things as they really are but how she wants to see them. By being 'in love,' she is, in a way, in a new dimension and is thinking 'we' instead of 'me'. She now defines herself as a part of something - a relationship. By investing her time, love, and future into this man, she is willing to rearrange her plans to include him in her life. These types of important decisions are made without him having been 'brought to court' to be proven worthy or unworthy by parties with a more objective perspective. She has willingly given him authority in her life without even knowing if he is capable of handling it.

Choosing to date leads to making a connection, which leads to becoming invested and allowing yourself to fall in love, when really a better term is 'jumping into love'. She has jumped into love without really knowing if he wants her love, is ready to accept love, or willing to give love back. When she gets hurt or angry at the man, she then goes back to her family and friends to tell them how he has hurt her and all she has had to endure and forgive. Then when the man comes around again, she allows him back in, while the family/friends are confused and frustrated by her making the same poor choices that leave her more broken than before.

Why? Why would a woman choose to date instead of enter into a courtship? Why trust her family and friends in all aspects of her life except love? Why think that family and friends do not have her best interest when it comes to the most precious aspect of life, her heart? It doesn't make much sense does it? It doesn't make sense that we would entrust our lives to our family and friends but not our hearts. What purpose would our loved ones have for steering us wrong when it comes to our heart? Why do women want to go out and jump into a relationship and then bring him to her loved ones for them to meet? It doesn't make sense.

What would happen if you were walking and you saw a stray puppy? It would look up at you and your heart would melt. You pick up the puppy and take it with you to the pet store. You buy it a collar and some great accessories. Then you take it to show your family and friends. Then one of them asks if you are allowed to have pets in your apartment complex. You don't know. You know that there are some regulations about it, but you are not sure if the puppy you picked up is the right breed and weight requirement to keep him in your apartment. Someone else asks if your rent will go up because of having a pet. You don't know, but your puppy is really cute. Your puppy explores the new location and starts to 'mark' the new environment. Unhappy, your friends and family complain about the puppy's behavior. You jump up and defend the puppy and quickly go to clean the mess up.

As you are cleaning, the puppy goes and starts to bite the furniture and tears holes into it. Annoyed, your family/friends complain again while you jump up and defend the behavior by mentioning that the puppy isn't accustomed to its new surroundings. The puppy then growls at an infant and you jump up, collect the puppy, and state that it's not used to strangers. One of your friends asks if your puppy has all its shots. Embarrassed that you have no idea, you state that you are taking it to get its shots updated first thing tomorrow. Frustrated that no one else seems to be as excited as you are to find such a great and cute puppy and that everyone seems to only want to focus on the negative, you choose to leave. You are annoyed that no one else was happy for you but you are certain that you are right and everyone else is wrong. You are now determined to make it work.

Doesn't make much sense does it? But many women choose to enter into a relationship entrusting another person with their heart and future without enough information and without trusting family/friends. This doesn't seem to make any more sense.

The problem is women chose to jump, not fall, into love. But you don't even know what you are jumping into. You don't know how deep the drop is. You don't know if you will have a soft or hard landing. You don't know if he is actually jumping with you, and you've already jumped. Why not wait and investigate what you are getting into before your heart has taken off. Think about courtship rather than dating. Think of some of the benefits to having someone that loves and can protect you screen the men that approach you before you become involved with them. Having this kind of protection will definitely ward off the men that don't want the responsibility of a real relationship, and it will further intrigue those that are. They see that you are valuable, and that difference demands a higher level of effort and sets you apart from other women.

From Price Tag To Priceless

Chapter Ten – Finders Keepers

One thing I want women to clearly understand is that you are the treasure! Women are the treasure. You are the thing that men want. You are the most valuable thing to men **when** you know your value. But you are the one that puts a clearance tag on yourself. How do you do this?

Instead of being the treasure to be found, you make yourself the treasure map! You tell men:

- how to find you
- what you like
- what you don't like
- how much is in your chest (i.e. your past)
- when you're available
- what he can get from you
- what you are willing to do for him
- how you can elevate him

You give him everything he needs to know about you **before** he even begins looking for you! Men are not as complex as women think they are. Men really are the hunters. They like to hunt and when you jump out and say "here I am", you have ruined it for him. You didn't make it a challenge, so he's no longer interested.

Think about it, when you were a kid playing hide-and-seek, would that game be any fun if the seeker went looking and everyone would jump out and say "here I am" – NO, it ruins the game. The person that would jump out instead of hiding until they were found wrecked the fun, and you didn't want them to play because what's the point?

The same is true in relationships. A man wants to approach a woman. He wants to talk to her and find out more about her at his pace – not hers. Instead of allowing the man to do the "digging", women jump out and say "here I am". And he's no longer interested because of giving him too much too soon and not allowing him to hunt.

***

Zack was at the club when he spotted a girl sitting at a table. He was about to walk up to her and ask if he could sit down when another girl walked up to him. "Hi. I'm Leslie, you want to dance?" she asked. He shook his head no, so she went on talking. "I'm so glad I came out tonight with my girlfriends. I really needed to unwind after the week I had. My boss was such a jerk, my boyfriend and I broke up, my kid got suspended from school, and my car broke down. It was just one thing after another, you know? Yeah, so when my girlfriends asked me to come out, I was so ready. What about you? Do you come here a lot?" He shook his head no and said, "I'm here with some friends, and I'm going to go find them, but have fun." He walked away and looked to see if the girl was still sitting at the table. She was. He walked up to her table and asked if he could sit down. She nodded her head yes and he sat down. "Hi I'm Zack, what's your name?" "Mary" she replied. "I noticed you've been sitting here for a while, don't you like the music?" he asked. She smiled and answered, "I like the music but my feet hurt from dancing so I'm just taking a break." Zack looked down at her shoes and saw her open toe strappy high heeled shoes and perfectly manicured toe nails. He smiled and said, "well I guess it's true." She looked at him puzzled and he went on to say, "beauty is pain." They both laughed at his corny line. "Why don't we give your beautiful feet a rest for two more songs and then dance the next song?" She nodded her head yes.

Women forget that men want to pursue them. He wants you to catch his eye and approach you the way he wants to but, when you ambush him, you throw him off track. Women too often try to make things happen!

Think of the treasure map. Men want to go on the adventure. They have the map and want to find the treasure. He wants to follow his map, find the X, dig, see the treasure chest, and then open the chest to see the treasure. He doesn't want to walk out his door and have you standing there. Looking for you is part of the pleasure. He enjoys the adventure. It's the journey to the destination that he wants.

A woman wants to be treasured but is too impatient to be found. She takes matters into her own hands and makes herself the treasure map. She gives him her map and he'll open her chest, but because she gave him her map, he wonders how many other men she's shown her map to. In his mind he wonders how many other men have seen, touched, and worn the gems and jewels in her chest. And she isn't precious to him anymore.

So stop jumping out and saying "here I am". Don't give a man the map to your heart. Just wait and let him find you. Give him time to find the map, go on the adventure, find the X, take out his shovel and dig, find your chest, open the lock, and treasure you.

Reclaim your value. No one can walk into a jewelry store and say "here's $0.99 give me a diamond." Stop putting yourself on clearance just so someone will take you.

You are a diamond, not a rhinestone. Don't give yourself away. Know your value and don't let yourself be taken for anything less than you're worth.

From Price Tag To Priceless

Chapter Eleven – Bonus Nuggets

- Lie VS. Omission
- Monogamy
- Right Person, Wrong Time
- Price Tag VS. Priceless
- Subcategories

Lie vs. Omission

Lie > fib; untruth; propaganda; story; falsehood

Omission > oversight; lapse; slip; exclusion; absence; leaving out; exception

Truth > fact; reality; certainty; honesty; accuracy; genuineness; legitimacy; integrity

You can also look at these three as:

lie = black

omission = gray

truth = white

This is a topic that causes much debate between women and men. Point blank, omission **does not equal** a lie.

The thing with omission is that, depending on the purpose of its use, it can cause problems in the relationship.

Omission of information, when used properly, is used to protect a loved one. However, the use of omission can be abused. When information is continually omitted, it can cross into the territory of lying very quickly.

In the case of cheating, the person doing the cheating is not omitting information; they are lying to keep the fact that they are cheating a secret.

With this information established, perhaps observing lying vs. omission in an example would be helpful to clearly determine when the use of each is appropriate/inappropriate.

***

Sandra and Neil had dated on and off for two years. Their relationship started off great with them enjoying spending more and more time together. In the beginning of the relationship, Sandra told Neil that she wanted to be a virgin when she got married because she wanted it to be special. Neil had been in sexual relationships in the past and, although it was refreshing to meet a woman with different standards, it was difficult for him to be in a relationship where his sexual needs were not being met.

After two months of dating, the desire became too much for Neil and he took the opportunity to have sex with a good friend of his that he used to date. He knew that he had messed up, and he didn't want to tell Sandra, but he knew he had to. After avoiding her calls for two days, he finally decided to call her. "Sandra, I'm sorry I haven't spoken to you for the last couple of days, but I've been busy working," Neil winced as he heard himself lie to her. "Oh I understand. Is anything wrong" she asked? He took a deep breath and went on. "Well, I'm sorry but it's a lot harder for me to be in a sexless relationship than I thought it would be, and I want to break-up" he said, as controlled as he could make his voice sound. He felt the back of his throat start to close up.

There was silence on the other end of the line while she was trying to process what she had just heard him say. She didn't know what to say and didn't have a chance to think of anything to say when he abruptly ended the phone call. Confused, she hung up the phone. Something didn't add up. It would have been different if they had talked about how he was having difficulty being in a sexless relationship, but he hadn't expressed that it was such a problem. She was supposed to meet some friends at the gym so she changed and went. Sandra got on the treadmill in between her two friends and started walking. One of her friends asked what was wrong, so she told them about the conversation she just had with Neil. They couldn't believe it either. They told her she was better off without him and continued to work out. Sandra couldn't help thinking that something wasn't right. As she came across the last 5 minutes of her workout, she felt the tears stream down her face. At first she thought it was sweat then she realized she was crying.

The next day after work, Sandra checked her phone, and she had a message from Neil. She listened to the message and then sat on her bed in disbelief. His voice sounded like he had been crying, and in the message he explained that he had sex with an ex-girlfriend, Jane. He said that it didn't mean anything to him. She lay on her bed and replayed the message over and over again. "I knew it. I knew there was something he wasn't telling me" she said. She cried herself to sleep that night.

After a while they began talking again as friends and eventually started dating again. Neil had many female friends and they all went out in groups. Sandra would go out with her friends and Neil would go out with his. At the end of the night, they would all end up at the same place. When Sandra would ask what friends he was with he usually said "oh the guys and some of their friends." He didn't bother to go through and name each guy and girl that was out with him, partially on purpose. He knew that she wouldn't be happy if he mentioned that Jane, the girl that he first cheated on her with, hung out with them. Jane had hung around their group of friends since he was 15 years old. He didn't want Sandra to worry or be upset because there wasn't anything for her to worry about anymore. He loved Sandra.

To recap, let's look at the lies vs. omissions:

- Neil said that he hadn't called because he was busy – Lie

- Neil said that he wanted to break up because it was harder for him to be in a sexless relationship than he thought it would be – Truth/Omission/Lie

    i. He told the truth about it being difficult for him to be in a sexless relationship
    ii. He omitted the fact that he had sex with someone else
    iii. He lied about the reason why he was breaking up with her > the fact that being in a sexless relationship wasn't the reason for the break-up; it was because he had cheated on her that he broke up with her

- Neil said that he had sex with an ex-girlfriend – Omission > he left out the fact that she was a person he had known from the time he was 15 which would tell Sandra that Jane wasn't just an ex-girlfriend, she was a person that was part of his circle of friends that he interacted with regularly

- Neil wouldn't name each person that he hung out with – Omission > he knew that Sandra would be bothered by the fact that Jane was around, but to him, Sandra didn't have anything to worry about because she was the one he loved, and he didn't want her to worry about him and Jane being in the same place

Finding out details that have been omitted can be difficult to deal with. The reason is that the assumption is made that one person was purposely hiding something from another person to benefit from it. However, it is more accurate that many times omission is used to prevent someone from being hurt further.

You have to be careful about what you say because many people make the bold statement that 'honesty is the best policy'. But is it really? If you are in a situation where you have been cheated on, there is a part of you that wants to know everything, every last detail. You want to know:

- What did you do?
- Who did you do it with?
- Why did you do it?
- Where did you do it?
- Was it better with that person?
- What was it about **me** that made you go to another person?
- Do you feel the same about them as you do about me?

- Do you love them?
- What were you wearing?
- What were they wearing?
- What did you say to them?
- What did they say to you?

And the questions never end. In your own quest for the 'truth', you end up hurting yourself. After a person gets cheated on and demands to know every detail, they then have to reconcile within themselves the information they just learned. Demanding to know every detail is like being cut by someone and then demanding that they pour salt and lemon juice into your open wound. Don't do it!

Use wisdom when dealing with this type of situation. The problem with demanding to know every detail is that it's never going to be enough, and, in the end, how will you benefit from it? Usually, it will cause more doubt and insecurity in you. Know the difference between a lie and an omission. In a heated discussion or a fight from learning about an omission, don't accuse him of lying because it's wrong. Both words cannot be used interchangeably because they simply don't mean the same thing.

Monogamy

Leland and Iris had been dating for a month. They weren't 'boyfriend and girlfriend' yet but were headed in that direction. Iris was different from the girls Leland had been involved with in the past, and he was enjoying getting to know her. He was drying off after his shower when he heard the doorbell ring. He looked at the clock and thought it was too early for Iris to be here, as his brother Scott answered the door. "Hey Melissa, he just got out of the shower. You want to watch T.V. while he gets ready?" Leland cringed as he heard his brother talking to Melissa. He didn't invite her over. What was she doing here? Leland was putting his shoes on when he heard the doorbell again. Scott got up from the couch and answered the door. "Hey Trina, Becky, Reese come in" he smiled, knowing that Leland was not going to be happy with all these girls being here and Iris on her way. Hearing Scott answer the door made Leland shake his head in confusion. What were all these girls doing here? Girls and friends in general were used to coming over to their house at all hours of the day, which hadn't been a big deal before, but now was starting to be problematic. Leland looked at his reflection one last time before heading downstairs. As he reached the last step on the stairs, the doorbell rang again. He answered the door and it was Carina. "Hi Leland, you want to go get something to eat?" He shook his head no and answered, "I'm actually on my way out." He hadn't opened the door all the way and she pushed her way in. She looked at all the girls in the house and walked past them, purposely not acknowledging them, as she sat by Scott, who was grinning ear to ear seeing the situation getting worse for Leland. He was about to close the door when he spotted Iris's car driving up the street. He didn't want Iris to walk into his house full of girls glaring at each other. Leland had slept with three of the girls in the house but wasn't committed to any of them. They were just friends who had sex when the opportunity presented itself. The girls knew of each other but didn't necessarily like each other. "Alright, I'm out," he yelled at Scott and the house full of girls as he shut the door behind him. He ran to meet Iris as she pulled up to the house and jumped into the car. "Hey, you look nice, let's go" he said. She looked at him a little surprised and responded. "Thanks you look nice, too, but I was going to park because I kind of need to use the bathroom" she said. Leland didn't want her to walk into his house full of girls and explain who they were or why they were there. He smiled at her and said, "we'll get to the movies quick, and I'd hate to miss the previews. Are you sure you can't make it?" She tilted her head as she thought and he continued "come on let's go, and I'll get you some candy for not peeing your pants." She laughed and pulled off. He laughed and thought in his head 'whew that was close!' After the movie, Leland called Scott while Iris was in the bathroom to see if the house was empty. To his dismay, the house was full of more people because it was the place to meet before going out. Iris walked out of the bathroom and over to Leland. "So, are we going to hang out at your house," she asked? "You know, it's a nice night, why don't we go by the river for a while?" He smiled and took her hand and led her out of the building.

***

At what point in a relationship are you expected to be monogamous? Are you expected to be monogamous when you start talking to each other and realize you are attracted to each other? Is it when a man and a woman become 'boyfriend and girlfriend'? Is it when they become engaged? Is it when they become married? Is it when they have been married and then have a child? Depending on who you ask, you will get different answers.

One answer that is easier to find uniformity in is that men expect women to be monogamous through each question/stage mentioned. In dating, there is a double standard (there always has been)! The double standard in dating is that men and women are judged differently.

If a man approaches a woman and they exchange numbers and then go on a date, he expects her to only be talking/dating/having sex with him. If he finds out that she is talking/dating/having sex with others, he feels betrayed, and most times she is re-categorized. If he learns that she has been with people he personally knows, it is even harder for him to deal with. It's key to remember that this process of judging a woman occurs before they have even gone onto the next stage of becoming 'boyfriend and girlfriend'. Some men go to great lengths to investigate the woman before even considering entering into the 'boyfriend/girlfriend' stage. He will ask his friends about the girl he is interested in, to see what she is known for. Is she a girl that goes home with men? Does she stay with her girlfriends, arriving and leaving with them? What sort of reputation does she have? He wants the answers to these questions before seriously thinking about making her his girlfriend. If she is in any way tainted, according to his standards, then he approaches the relationship with caution. He either re-categorizes her as a friend, friend with benefits, a booty call girl, a one night-stander, or he will choose to leave her alone completely. He rarely decides to give her the benefit of the doubt. He is curious and wants to find out why she has a reputation, so he will investigate to hear her side. If he can reconcile the responses she gives him, then he may proceed in getting to know her better, but with the first glance he gets of the 'old reputation,' he is quick to disconnect himself from her.

    A woman, however, tends to be a bit more forgiving when the situation is reversed. She will rationalize that they were not committed to each other and therefore what happened in the past stays in the past, and she is able to move forward in the relationship with the man.

If or when Iris found out about what happened the day she went to pick up Leland and he had a house full of past sexual acquaintances, she could rationalize the fact that Leland and her had just started dating and were not in a committed relationship. So, in essence, he had not cheated on her. If, however, the situation was reversed, Leland would not continue to see Iris as a possible girlfriend. She might be reclassified as someone he would have sex with when the opportunity presented itself, but he would not want her as a girlfriend. The only exception (and I mean ONLY exception) for men is when they have had a huge crush on the woman and are willing to excuse her past to have the opportunity to be with her. This rarely happens, and it is even rarer that it ends up in a long-term relationship.

With all of this in mind, monogamy becomes a complicated issue. First, there are the questions mentioned above regarding when one is expected to be monogamous.

Second, what is considered monogamous and non-monogamous? What is classified as non-monogamous varies depending on whom you ask. Many men, for instance, don't consider oral sex as cheating or being non-monogamous. Interestingly enough, the same men would not tolerate having another man performing oral sex on his woman; ergo, another double standard.

As you meet a man and begin the phases of getting to know each other, you can prevent being disillusioned by being more proactive. As you are getting to know him, know the kinds of questions to ask and let him answer the questions and pay attention to how he answers them. You could ask him, "so what are we doing?" To which he might answer "getting to know each other." And you would follow that up with something like, "and how many other people are you currently getting to know?" Pay close attention to see if he laughs. His laughter can be more revealing than an actual answer.

If he says something like "what do you mean?" this could be a question to purposely divert/distract you, to which you would answer. "I mean you are the only person I am currently 'getting to know' by talking on the phone and going out or hanging out with. So, are you 'getting to know' others while getting to know me?" It's important to not be too specific with your answers, which allows him to provide you with his own explanations/responses. If you are too specific, he may tend to either nod his head, laugh, or just seem to agree with your own response. In other words, he allows you to answer your own question in a way or with an answer that you want to hear, while not ever really outright answering your question.

Things to be aware of:

- Him answering your questions with nonverbal responses (head nods, laughs, lifting his eyebrows, smiles, shoulder shrugs, etc.)

- Him diverting from your questions (by laughing them off or saying something like "What? You're funny") and never really answering your questions

- Him giving you a response that really isn't an answer or a response that is very vague like, "I'm just having fun getting to know you." (What does "having fun" mean to him and how many other girls is he "having fun" with in addition to you?)

Things you can ask him (in the early stages when you are not yet committed):

- What does monogamy mean to you?

- How do you or what do you define as a sexual act?

- Do you think oral sex is sex?

- How do you define cheating?

- At what point do you expect a girl to be monogamous with you?(if he doesn't understand the question, you can go through the stages mentioned above: early stages of dating, boyfriend/girlfriend, engaged, marriage, or when you have children?)

Asking these kinds of questions serves multiple purposes. On one hand, it allows you to learn from his perspective on the questions. On the other hand, the questions are arousing enough to be considered flirtatious. The purpose of asking these types of questions is that you get to find out if the two of you are on the same page instead of just assuming that you are. When you assume and then find out that it's not the case, you get hurt. It is also important to note, that you ask these kinds of questions as nonchalantly as possible. You don't want him to feel like he is being interrogated, and you don't want to come off as being paranoid or overzealous because it will probably scare him off. A big mistake women make is assuming too much without actually asking and hearing his perspective. Too often you find out that the two of you are on different pages when a conflict arises.

Right Person, Wrong Time

What happens when you meet the right person but at the wrong time? The right time requires for both parties to be:

a. Emotionally mature
b. Financially situated
c. Desiring a committed relationship

Many people will want all three things listed, but they want them in the future and are not ready for all three in the present time; hence, wrong timing. It's difficult for a person to say that they want all three things but are not ready for it. It takes really knowing themselves to be able to say that they aren't ready.

Emotionally mature

For men, this requires separating himself from his family/friends and being ready to start his own family with a wife. For women, this requires letting go of childish fantasies, fairy-tale endings and happily ever after that aren't real. If these fantasies are your measuring stick, then you will always end up disappointed, and you will place unrealistic expectations on men. Books are not the only culprit in ruining women's view on relationships/romance; songs and movies have also done their fair share of damage as well. Just because you read, hear, or see a particular type of relationship situation does not mean you should compare to or desire that situation.

The problem with comparing situations is that, if you look at another relationship and compare it to yours, the factors affecting the situations are never identical, so there is no comparison. Seeing another couple and desiring that type of situation is completely incorrect because it's like looking at a photograph. All you see is what is right before you, but you don't see what it took to get to that point. If you knew what it took to get to that point, you may not find that situation as desirable.

<u>Financially situated</u>

Men are strategists, and they calculate what needs to be done to achieve the things they want to achieve. In becoming financially situated, a man is aware of what he needs to get before committing to a relationship. He has to have a job, car, house, be out of debt, have enough money to be the provider, and enough money for entertainment. A man does not want to make a commitment and be responsible for a woman if he does not have things in order.

Women are analyst and romantics. She wants to build and grow together. She wants to be his helpmate. She doesn't think there is anything wrong with the man moving from his parent's house to her house. She wants to be equal partners and bring their assets together to build.

She gets her feelings hurt when he doesn't want to build with her, and she emasculates him when she insists on him doing things her way. Pay attention to a man's position. Listen to what he says, and, if he doesn't have most of the things in order that are listed, then he isn't ready. There is a reason for him to do things on his time. He has a blueprint. Don't make him abandon his plan and take steps that he isn't ready for; it can cause so much damage in your relationship.

<u>Desiring a committed relationship</u>

Umm this is a tricky one. For the most part, people eventually want to have a committed relationship. The problem is that it's more in the future than in the present. For men, it's more abstract than concrete. So to him, it's a 'someday' and not 'today'.

If the both of you are not on the same page with this factor, it does cause problems because it confuses women. She doesn't understand why he would put off what he says he wants when it's right in front of him.

So if a man tells a woman that he is not ready, there isn't a big mystery to find out what he's really saying - he just came out and said it. Women over analyze this comment when there is nothing to analyze; take it at face value – he's just not ready.

If a man tells you he isn't ready to be in a committed relationship, you have a couple of options:

a) End the relationship and go on living your life
b) Give up what you really want and keep the man on whatever terms he'll have you

Option a:

Remember that old saying that goes something like "if you set it free and it doesn't come back then it didn't belong to you, but, if you set if free and it comes back then it was meant to be." There is definitely wisdom in that saying. If a man tells you that he is not ready to be in a committed relationship and you choose to end the relationship, what do you lose?

The relationship is over. You go your way and he goes his. Then you go through your routine of getting over an ended relationship. You have your girls' night outs, go to your comfort foods, watch movies that either make you cry or empower you, and you go shopping. You may avoid the places you used to go to when you were in the relationship, go over your ended relationship in your head of what you did vs. what he did. Maybe you jump back into dating to get over the last relationship. Basically, you do whatever has worked for you in the past to 'self-medicate' and get over the relationship.

Eventually, you feel better and are either back on track or may be on a new track. You are focused on what you want and how to get it. You continue to grow and develop, experiencing and living your life.

As the two of you grow separately, you aren't going to be the same people that you were before, and it may be the case that you become "the one that got away". Or after some time, your paths may cross again; but remember, you and he are not the same people you were before, so don't expect things to be the same.

Option b:

"But I love him." When you want to be in a committed relationship with a man who does not want to be in a committed relationship and you choose to stay at whatever capacity he'll have you, you are in for a difficult road. The thing that is clear is that he doesn't want what you want, and to keep *some* of what you want, you compromise yourself.

Let's go through step by step what happens when you choose Option b.

- First there is a conversation that occurs where you and the man realize that you want two different things
- Then you decide you don't want to be without him
- You have a discussion with him and he tells you he doesn't want to be in a committed relationship
- You ask why not?
- He goes through his reasons (he might use one of the following or something similar)
    - I just got out of a serious relationship, and I'm not ready to go back into another one
    - I just want to enjoy meeting different people
    - I just want to keep it light

- - You know I want to have fun, and, if I meet someone and she's into me and I'm into her, hey, we're both adults. And, if we hook up (have sex), I don't want to feel guilty about it I'd rather be honest.

- You feel hurt and a bit rejected and you may choose to leave at this point and decide that maybe the two of you can still be friends

- After a few days you have replayed the conversation in your head, and you decide to 'stay friends' so you do something to reach out to him
  - You may call him and invite him out as friends to do something like have lunch/watch a movie/hang out
  - You might just show up somewhere you know he will be and start the 'friend-relationship'
    - The key thing about this step is that the conscious/subconscious level about what you are doing varies, but, if you are really being honest with yourself, you are making first contact, **not** him. You have made yourself the hunter, and your category has changed from Main to 3rd

- At this point, because you are reaching out to him, you are positioning yourself to become a friend with benefits

- He then takes you up on your offer and becomes intimate with you (emotionally and sexually)

- Soon the two of you are in a routine, similar to the one you used to have when you were first dating
    - You talk on the phone
    - You hang out
    - You do 'date' type things
    - You have sex

- Then he has sex with someone else

- You find out and confront him

- He reminds you that you are not in a committed relationship
    - He points out that he told you he did not want to be in a committed relationship – that he was honest about what he wanted
    - He states that he thought "we were two consenting adults. If we wanted to have sex with each other, that was it." But maybe you can't handle that kind of relationship

- You leave hurt and angry

- After a few days he calls

- He makes his 'grand gesture'
    - This can be something small or large but most importantly it is something that reflects your relationship and is personal to you (flowers, cooking for you, etc.)

- And the cycle begins again

This cycle continues until one of you decides that you're done. The longer you choose to repeat this cycle, the more you invest, and it becomes harder to walk away from the relationship each time. Women who choose to continue in this pattern can end up investing years into this relationship.

A good question to ask is why?

- Why would you want to give up what you want – a committed relationship
- Why would you want to share the person you love emotionally/sexually/spiritually with other women
- Why would you want to value a relationship more than yourself
- Why don't you believe that the way you love a person is the way you deserve to be loved
- Why do you sell yourself short
- Why believe that a poor relationship is better than no relationship

Consequences:

If you are in an Option b type of situation, please know that too much compromise can really hurt you. When you choose to end this relationship, it will take some time to get back to knowing what you really want and who you really are because of compromising so much for the relationship.

If he ends the relationship, it's a hard break-up to get over, especially once you hear that he is in a committed relationship with his new Main.

When choosing Option b, you run the risk of continuing the cycle and end up hurting each other repeatedly. Being repeatedly hurt affects trust and love. It may be more difficult to heal than you can imagine. Because of not being able to forgive and heal, it may be difficult to be in a relationship with him.

So how do you know if it is the right person but the wrong time? First, look back at what has he said to you in the past and how has he treated you throughout the relationship. Has he treated you like a Main in public? Have you acted like a Main or have you done things that would re-categorize you? If he has told you that he loves you and wants to be with you someday, but he's not ready right now, then you have more to gain by ending the relationship then and there.

Really look at where you and he are at this stage in life. Are the two of you emotionally mature, financially situated, and mutually desiring to be in a committed relationship? If not, you can end the relationship and continue to develop and grow separately. Then when the two of you are both ready, you can come back together or maybe the paths you have chosen will lead you to a different and more suitable person.

>It's important to know:
>Who are you?
>Do you like yourself?
>What's important to you?
>What do you want in a relationship?
>What do you not want in a relationship?
>What are your deal breakers?

Know the answers to these questions *before* getting into a relationship. Know what you have to offer before coming to the table to play. It's your heart, treat it well. If you don't, then who will?

Price Tag VS. Priceless

If you want to be in a healthy relationship, it is important to know what your standards are. You must use wisdom to be sure that your standards don't become price tags. There is a difference between having standards and placing a price tag on yourself. Examples of standards are things like, does the man:

- Love God
- Respect you
- Have a job – able to be a provider (not *potentially* but is right now able to)
- Is trustworthy/honest
- Have the means to own a home or already owns a home

<u>Love God</u>

If a man loves God, then he will be able to truly love you. Why? If a man has the ability to believe and love a *Being* that is not physically present the way you are, he is much more capable of loving a person that is physically present. Loving God teaches the man to submit to something other than himself. By his submission, he opens himself up to being vulnerable to God, and God rebuilds the man with another level of ability to express love in a way that is unselfish. Now to be clear, loving God does not mean that the man is perfect (there is no such thing), but it does mean that a man that loves God is able to go to God and ask for the ability to love another person the way that God loves him. A great definition of love can be found in the Bible in 1 Corinthians 13:4-13.

Now, I'm saying that it is a great definition of love, yet attaining it is pretty improbable. If you are willing to aspire to that kind of love, then that is the definition that I suggest you look up to have the best explanation of what love is. A man may say that he believes in God, but look at how he leads his life. Does he demonstrate that he loves God in his everyday life or is it only on Sundays, or is it only during Christmas and Easter? Watch and see if what he says matches what he does. If he is a man that loves God, it will show by his actions. By knowing that he can submit himself to God, he will be able to treasure you the way God treasures you. He will be able to treat you like a precious, priceless treasure because that is how God teaches and allows him to see you-the way God sees you.

<u>Respect you</u>

The definition of respect, can be very different to different people. For the purpose of this chapter, my definition of respect is that you are not called out of your name. By this I mean that you are not called something that you are not. If a person calls you a name to put you down, knock you down a peg – that's not love. Respect also means that someone has a high opinion of you. How can someone who has a high opinion of you call you something to purposely cause you hurt? Respect also involves someone seeing your value and honoring that value. As I said before, you can't expect to go into a jewelry store and demand a diamond for the price of a rhinestone; it just won't happen. The jeweler knows the value of a diamond and demands the appropriate value. Do you know your value? Do you demand your value or let yourself be taken for the price of a rhinestone?

<u>Have a job</u>

It is important to see a situation for how and what it really is. Women too often see what they want to see instead of seeing what really is. A man having a job demonstrates important qualities like responsibility, faithfulness, consistency, and dependability. If a man exercises these types of qualities then he is able to provide for you and a future family. Having a job demonstrates ability instead of capability. Too often women believe in things like capability, possibility, prospective, and opportunity. You know what the problem with this is? There is always a 50% chance that he will become what you believe he can be, but there is also a 50% chance that he will not become what you believe he can be and the choice is his to make, not yours. You chose to be in a situation, always waiting for him to choose what you would like for him to choose, but it is his choice to make to be better and your choice to stick around to see if he will.

Is trustworthy/honest

Why would you entrust your heart to a man that is not trustworthy or honest? It sounds ridiculous, but it is very common. What attributes are associated with being trustworthy? Things like dependable, constant, honorable, faithful, honest, responsible, and unfailing. Typically, you meet a man and assume he is trustworthy/honest until he does something or you hear something that says otherwise. So many times you don't find out that he is not trustworthy until you get hurt. Sometimes you become involved with a man and then later find out that in the past he may not have been trustworthy or honest and then you have to see if he has changed. He will tell you that he has, but you must look at his life, and how he lives it. People make mistakes and those mistakes don't dictate who they will be. If you learn from your mistakes and purposely make efforts to avoid making those mistakes again, you can change. A person that has been unfaithful, dishonest, or untrustworthy can change, but they have to make that choice to change.

<u>Have the means to own a home or already owns a home</u>

There is a reason why I state this item in two ways. There are people that, because of their culture, believe that they are to live with their family until they are married, so there is no need for them to buy a home until they marry. However, they have the ability to buy a home when it is time to. Sometimes women are disappointed to learn that a grown man lives in his family's home not, understanding that his cultural norm or family dynamic says that the children live at home until married. He may already own a home of his own, which demonstrates that he is responsible, disciplined, and dependable. He has the ability to work for what he wants and take care of it, which means he is able to be a good provider for a wife and family.

These five things are great standards to look for in men that approach you wanting to become involved in a relationship with you. All demonstrate the opportunity for him to show you that he is actively taking care of himself and able to take care of you (someone else). Each item demonstrates that he is actually doing these things, not that he is just capable of it.

How does a standard become a price tag? This occurs when a woman begins to judge a man's character by materialistic things. Making statements like "a real man would..." or "if you loved me you would..." Understand that equating a man's character to materialistic things is unfair and erroneous. The two things don't mean the same thing, manhood and materialistic items; they cannot be substituted for each other. Yet, women make statements that try to make it seem as though he's less than a man if he doesn't provide the things that she demands.

Standards make a woman priceless. A woman with high standards will be treated with a different level of value because she knows her value and becomes priceless. Materialism attaches the price tag to the woman that she writes across herself, and she is eventually treated as an object that is bought. Once she is bought, she becomes a possession to either be treasured or mistreated, and, usually, she is mistreated due to the price tag that she has set. The priceless woman is treasured, but the price tag woman eventually loses her value; she depreciates while the priceless woman continues to be valuable.

When men investigate and realize that your standards are really price tags, they quickly re-categorize you. You went from a Main to a 3rd, or you stayed a Main but he won't see you as an equal partner. You become a possession because he has to pay to be with you. Once he realizes you have placed a price tag on yourself, he will do one of two things: either he will continue to pay to keep you happy, or he will begin to treat you like an object that he owns. If he treats you like an object he owns, eventually he will resent the situation and then take it out on you. He'll demand things, and, because he's paying, 'put out or get out' becomes the mentality. But the key thing to remember is that you (the woman) started the situation by turning your standards into price-tags.

Some women believe they are priceless but unwittingly set a price tag on themselves, which determines how a man categorizes them. For example, a woman believing that she is priceless tells a man that she is not the kind of woman that is taken to the dollar theatre. She doesn't eat at fast-food restaurants on dates. She doesn't want to have a price limit set when she is on a dinner date. She wants to travel so a man that she is with has to provide certain things, and she clearly states the kinds of things she expects. By having a checklist of things that she requires in order for her to be with a man, the checklist becomes price tags.

Price Tag sayings:

- You can't afford me/this
- I only buy things from catalogs
- Name brands
- Seasonal wardrobe
- Fast-food isn't a date
- One of a kinds
- I need a vehicle no older than two years
- Upgrade
- If it isn't real then I don't wear it
- Shopping spree without a spending limit

Remember, men look at women like they look at cars. He has the Clunker, the one that gets him from A to B. The Winter Beaters the one he won't take out in the summer but will shack up with all winter. The Drop-Top Convertible that he wants to be seen with in the summer,

summer flings. Then there is the classic that never loses its value, that he continues to invest his time and money into. He is proud to show her off, protects her, and wants to keep her. Losing her would hurt him too much.

Strive to be a classic. Be a person of good character with standards that demonstrate your value, and you will be cherished by the one that sees who you really are and how much you are worth.

Subcategories

You know how you can change the entire look of an outfit by merely accessorizing differently? Well, that is kind of how subcategories are created. These subcategories consist of different choices women make that change how a man categorizes them. As a man spends more time getting to know a woman, he begins to attach more subcategories to her based on her actions, which can become extremely complicated!

The Zebra

The Zebra is a woman that carries herself like a Main. She dresses modestly. She represents herself very well verbally, doesn't say things that are inappropriate. She even attends church regularly. So why is she a Zebra? Well, what happens with this woman is that, although she looks and acts like a Main, she does something, which for a man, changes her status. She has premarital sex. The man needs to reconcile the contradiction before him. She looks like a

Main, and for the most part, acts like a Main, but when he tries to have sex with her, she doesn't object. So is she white with black stripes or is she black with white stripes? The fact that the Zebra seems like a good woman in most of the areas that a man is looking for, and although he is the one that initiates having sex with her, the fact that she consents, changes her category if a man does not want to commit to her. This is because after they have sex, he then wonders "is she really a good woman?" Or "how many other guys did she have sex with but claimed she was a 'good girl'?" So the very act that the man initiates, she accepts, then becomes the reason that he turns around and judges the woman and she is re-categorized.

The Tease

This is the woman that many times doesn't really do anything physically sexual with a man but she plays with him. She says things that are highly laced with sexual innuendos. She may say things for shock value. Or ask a man questions that are inappropriate/sexual. At times there is physical touching like hugging, grinding/dancing; she might sit on his lap. But the actual physical contact may vary from none to a lot. The thing is, it doesn't matter if she touches him or not, she is still placed in the same category. A Tease is automatically a subcategory of a 3rd. Women that find themselves in this place often don't understand why they aren't in a committed relationship. They wonder why they are often overlooked as they see the women around them in and out of relationships. The men that come across the Tease at first don't mind the interactions between them, but once they realize that the woman is a Tease, they don't like to be played. So he may spend time entertaining the Tease but is quick to move on and talk to another female once he finds one that catches his eye.

***

Mia was looking around the club to see if Paul was already there when she spotted him by the bar. She smiled and he nodded his head, acknowledging that he saw her. Mia had her favorite black dress on, the one that hugged every curve just right. She sat back on her stool knowing that Paul would buy her a drink and bring it to her. Paul made his way to her, bringing her a drink, and sat in the stool by Mia. She leaned in and gave him a kiss on the cheek, her usual greeting. They sipped on their drinks as she leaned in and brushed his hair behind his ear. A familiar song came on, and he grabbed her hand and led her to the dance floor. They danced with their bodies pressed close up against each other. Following her lead, Paul began to hug Mia tightly in his arms as his hands slowly moved down Mia's back. As his hands began to go down further and further, Mia quickly pulled away from him and smiled. She shook her head 'no' and walked off the dance floor. Paul let out a sigh and walked off the dance floor towards the bar. Frustrated, he wanted another drink after going through the same old routine Mia put him through. As he ordered his drink at the bar, he looked over at a girl sitting at an empty table. She wasn't aware anyone was looking at her as she nodded her head to the music. She was pretty, and he couldn't help but smile as she seemed to be in her own little world as she moved to the beat. He took his drink as he walked over to her table. He stood there for a moment while she continued to enjoy the music, oblivious to his presence. Suddenly, she looked up and saw him staring at her. Embarrassed, she smiled and blushed. He smiled back at her and asked if she would like to dance. "I'm sorry, but I can't" she replied. She saw the disappointed look on his face and she continued, "I would like to, but it's my turn to watch the purses while my friends dance. But you can sit if you'd like, and then when one of them comes back, we can dance." He sat down and introduced himself. "I'm Paul." She shook his hand and replied "hi, I'm Dina." They started talking and getting to know each other while they waited for her friends to come relieve her from guarding the purses. Mia realized that Paul hadn't come back with her drink and started looking around for him. She spotted him sitting with another girl talking and laughing with her. Mia hadn't seen this girl before and wondered who she was. Just then, a song came on that she always danced to with Paul, but he wasn't getting up from the table. Then a group of girls went to the table and blocked her view. Then she saw Paul stand up, so Mia got up to meet him when she saw him leading the girl he was talking to onto the dance floor. She straightened out her dress to try and play off that she had gotten up for nothing then sat back down. As Mia watched from the table, Paul danced the next song and then the one after that. She opened her purse to see if she had any money, but she didn't. Mia was so used to having Paul buy her drinks that she rarely brought money to the club other than the cover charge to get in the club. She sighed as she continued to watch Paul dance with this new girl; it was like he forgot all about her, and she didn't like it.

The Beauty Queen

The Beauty Queen is extremely appealing and catches the man's eye immediately. As he looks at her, he wonders how high-maintenance is she. In his mind he thinks someone that physically attractive is used to receiving special treatment, and he doesn't know if he wants to put in all the work it would take to be in a relationship with her. But he would still like to walk into a place with her by his side. So the Beauty Queen then becomes a subcategory of a Main. He will approach her and have her by his side as long as she will be there without him having to work too hard.

The Seed Planter

This person does what the title says, plants seeds. The seeds they plant are words or ideas that open the door for men to know "just in case" the opportunity presents itself, the things she likes done to her and things she likes to do. Oh, and just so you know, those 'seeds' that she shares the men are not kept secret! Men tell other men what's been said, and they will also tell other women. So, something that was meant to serve a particular purpose of letting a man know what you like and what you do ends up becoming a way for other people to judge you. When a woman plays this role, she ultimately does herself the most damage. She thinks, on some level, that she is looking out for herself, but what she is really doing is short-changing herself. Whether or not she does anything physical with the men doesn't matter; she plants the seeds, and she is automatically categorized as a 3rd. Many times a seed planter will come across a few men that are in a "man-talk" conversation and jumps in. A "man-talk" conversation is when they are telling an account of their sexual escapades to which other men are trying to challenge their story and discount them by asking if the woman was drunk or find some other element to lessen the man's game ability. She may join in, but usually what she will do is pull the man that she wants to plant seeds in aside and start to talk about *her* sexual escapades. After she is done telling her story, she ends by asking a question like, "that doesn't make me a whore right?" She makes this comment while she laughs to lighten the mood, but, on some levels, she wants the man that she just planted seeds in to confirm that what she is doing isn't considered "whorish". Being put in an awkward position, the man either joins in laughing and shaking his head no, not able to tell her the truth about what he really thinks about the information he has just heard. After the conversation, he goes on to tell other men or women the information he has been told. So, he not only judges her, but he gives others the opportunity to do so as well. And just as a point of reference, seed planters do not only plant seeds that are explicitly sexual. Sometimes the seeds are statements like "you see, that's why you and I could never date because…" The seed that she is planting is that she has thought of the man in a relationship with her. When this happens the man usually goes to a friend and says something like, "yeah she said the weirdest thing, she said she could never date me because… what was that?" Whether the comments or 'seeds' are sexual or not, it makes a man think about the friendship/relationship. An important thing to remember is that he doesn't keep the learned information to himself, he shares it. Be careful what you share and how you share it. Information that you want to be private won't stay private because there is no real commitment between the two of you, so there is no obligation for him to protect you. Seed Planters are usually a subcategory of a 3rd because the actions they take is very purposeful. The tactics they utilize are viewed as manipulative or crafty because they are attempting to create an atmosphere of possibility but not guarantee.

The Dumper/T-M-I

Although the title of this subcategory may sound harsh, it means that she is the woman that dumps too much information (T-M-I) about herself too soon. She quickly divulges too much information way too soon, and this is the main reason why a man won't commit to her; she scares him off. It's like she comes to the table to play a hand of cards, and as soon as she has all of her cards, she lays them on the table to be seen before the game has even started. The type of information she freely gives can vary; it can be any of the following topics:

- How her last relationship ended
- Any information about her past partners
- Complaints about job/career
- Complaints about baby-daddy drama
- Information about children
- Elicit sexual information
- I love you / I like you (saying these statements too soon)

She provides the man with personal information, and he is not in a relationship with her. This bombardment of information is overwhelming to the man. He doesn't know what to do with it and it catches him off guard and then scares him away. Because the Dumper/T-M-I freely provides him with information without him seeking it, he knows that if he becomes involved with her, it will be more intense for her than it would be for him. She would be more invested, and he would feel pressured. To avoid feeling pressured, he usually keeps this woman at bay and categories her as a 2nd. He doesn't want to get involved in a sexual relationship because he knows that she wants and expects more than he desires to invest.

***

Mark was reading his book when he suddenly felt like someone was watching him. He looked up and saw a woman staring at him. She quickly looked away, embarrassed at having been caught staring at him. She was attractive, so he smiled at her. She was holding a book in her hands, and he motioned for her to come over to sit at his table. She smiled and walked towards him. When she got to the table he said, "I noticed you were checking out these chairs, not that I blame you. They are comfortable and perfect for reading in. Please see for yourself." He motioned for her to sit in the chair across the table from him. She nodded her head in agreement and sat down. She was relieved that he made a joke about catching her staring at him and placed her book down on the table. He glanced at her book and saw that it was a relationship self-help book. He began to wonder if he made a mistake by asking her to join him. He smiled at her and quickly picked up his book and tried to get back to reading. "Thank you for inviting me to join you. I'm Wendy," she said as she extended her hand. He looked up from his book and shook her hand, "nice to meet you Wendy, I'm Mark." He waited and looked at her for what he thought was an appropriate amount of time before getting back to his book. He noticed that she hadn't picked her book back up. "So, do you come here often," she asked? He nodded yes. "I haven't been in this bookstore before, but I like it, it's nice," Wendy said as she looked around the store. "I guess it's because I never really thought I had time to just relax and read, you know?

Actually, now that Billy and I aren't together, I have a lot of free time, and I just don't know what to do with myself." Mark let out a sigh. In his head he already knew that he had made a colossal mistake by talking to Wendy. "Billy and I were planning on getting married, but it didn't work out. Have you ever been engaged?" Mark shook his head no and put his book down so that he wouldn't come off as rude. He knew this was going to be a long conversation, and he wouldn't have much luck getting back to his reading today. He started to think of ways he could get out of this conversation without being too insensitive; he really didn't want to be part of this conversation any more. Maybe if he got a phone call, oh but he remembered he turned his ringer off when he started reading. Then he realized that Wendy had been talking while he was thinking. He had no idea what she had been saying when he tuned back in. "You know, I mean, who does that? I don't know what I was thinking! I mean, it's like up to this point I've been like a loser magnet. Guys just don't want to commit, and I have done everything, like I have put 150% into all my relationships, and they just never work out. I heard about this book and knew I had to read it because I am totally lost and don't want to be! Mark, you are such a great listener! I feel like I can tell you just about anything. Weird right? I mean, I know we just met, but I just feel so close to you." Wendy smiled at him and sat back. Mark had no idea what just happened. He smiled back at her, knowing that he had had enough. "Yeah, wow. Ah listen I'm sorry but I have to go, but it was nice meeting you and good luck with everything." Mark said as he got up from his seat, gathering his things and quickly walked out. Wendy sat stunned. She wasn't sure what had just happened. They were having such a great conversation, and then he just left. She didn't even get to give him her phone number. Dina sat back, took a deep breath and shrugged it off. She picked up her book and started to read.

The Independent/Dependent

Depending on how she expresses her independence determines the category a woman is placed, in which can easily change. If a woman presents herself as a very independent woman who wants to be in a committed relationship, she is then categorized as a Main. However, if a woman who presents herself as an independent woman who doesn't want to be in a committed relationship but wants to have individuals to have a sexual relationship with, she is categorized as a 3rd. What usually eventually happens is that this woman develops feelings of ownership with the person she regularly has sex with. (I use the word 'regularly' very broadly.) In this instance, 'regularly' doesn't necessarily mean that they have sex on a regular basis, like nightly. 'Regularly' can mean that both people have an understanding that whenever they would like to have sex with each other, they will. Then the man may meet a new woman that he wants to spend more time with exclusively, and the Independent woman comes around. She is used to their usual set-up and is not pleased to find that he has changed. Knowing that the situation that she was used to has changed, and not by her, she begins to be territorial. Because of the fact that the situation of their involvement is different, again because of him making the change, she becomes Dependent. Feeling that she has been somehow wronged, she expresses her dissatisfaction for how the man has changed their prior relationship arrangement. The Dependent characteristics manifest themselves as: jealous, angry, hurt, and territorial. Often he labels her as a 'psycho'. The problem is that when the relationship started, it was based on a particular understanding or arrangement, and when that was changed by the man, the woman felt wronged. But their situation was not based on exclusivity, so she never had any 'rights' to him. As sex is done on a regular basis, it becomes less casual and feelings begin to develop. Those feelings may be love but can be more about connection. When the connection is broken without both people deciding to do so mutually, then something feels broken or incomplete. The other person feels like they haven't been consulted and believe they are owed an explanation. When a man encounters the Independent woman and investigates to see if she is a Main or 3rd category, he then decides whether or not he will become involved with the woman. If she is Main material, and he does not want to be in a committed relationship, he may choose to not become involved. If she is 3rd material, he then can weigh the pros and cons of getting involved with her. Although the cons (in many cases) outweigh the pros, many men don't take the hurt they can cause these women into account when they have the opportunity to have sex with them. The hurt they cause is/was not necessarily done intentionally. In this situation the woman feels hurt and angry, while the man is upset that the woman blames him for hurting her. She is holding him accountable for a responsibility he never agreed to. Both the man and woman in this situation end up without even a friendship. They started out on the same path but went in two different directions and both end up dissatisfied with the outcome. The hurt caused in the situation can be too much for the friendship to be maintained.

The above subcategories are some of the categories linked to the original Main, 2nd, and 3rd categories, and as time goes by, new subcategories are created as society changes how relationships are labeled. For instance, 20 years ago, there was no such thing as 'sexting,' but now with cell phones and the internet, these technological developments have brought about new labels and actions. As with everything else, actions have consequences. You have to start realizing that the actions you take will either impact you positively or negatively. The key is to stop, look at your past choices and the places that they led to, evaluate whether you want to make a change, and then be proactive about the choices you make. By taking responsibility for what you have chosen to do, you are able to hold yourself accountable and hopefully make better choices.

From Price Tag To Priceless

Chapter Twelve – Wives

After you've said "I do," the real work begins of being a loving married couple. From the first date up to the wedding, you have probably gone through a rollercoaster of emotions. You've had the fantastic highs of getting butterflies when he called or walked into a room. And you've no doubt probably had some lows when the two of you faced conflicts. But now you have him, and you have to learn how to be married. It might come easy or it might take some adjustments, but, eventually, you fall into your new roles and routines.

Your new routines may involve work, personal development, career development, entertainment, maintaining a household, raising children, going to church, cooking, cleaning, shopping, yard work, family events, seeing friends, and, oh yeah, your relationship. With so much to do, it can easily become overwhelming, and you may not be able to do all the things you want or need to do. Unfortunately, your husband many times is the one that gets the least of your attention.

Why does your husband end up with less of your attention? Well, sometimes he is taken for granted because he is the one you started this new life with, and you expect him to always be there. But after being neglected, he begins to long to feel connected. And you know there are women that cross his path everyday that offer a connection.

So, how do you stay connected so that he doesn't look for others to connect with? Well, there is a reason for all three positions.

Throughout this process, we've looked at three categories (Main, 2nd, and 3rd) in which women are classified. The reason there are three positions is so that a wife can aspire to become all three. A woman that a man desires to marry is a person that stimulates him mentally, emotionally, and physically.

As a Main, she is the person that he is proud to introduce to his family and friends. A wife is the person he sees himself building a life with. She is the person that he longs to spend time with. He invests a lot of time thinking about his Main. Being with you makes him aspire to be the best man that he can be.

As a 2nd, a wife is supposed to be his best-friend. In the role of 2nd, you are the one that he shares his doubts and dreams with. He is able to open up and be vulnerable with the 2nd. He shares so much with her and doesn't fear that she will judge him or think less of him. He needs this safe space to be himself without consequence. In the 2nd position, you have to provide that environment that feels safe to him. If you don't develop this relationship, he will find it somewhere else. But, as his wife, you should be his confidant. Warning! Criticizing him, being overly sensitive to what he shares, and judging him deteriorates the safe space that a 2nd provides. If you respond in this way, he will eventually stop opening up to you and find someone he can talk to freely about what he thinks, feels, fears, and dreams.

So, how do you create or recreate your 2nd position if you don't play this role in your relationship? It will take work to build this role up. You have to construct this safe space that takes time to build. He has to be able to trust that if he opens up to you, he won't be judged. You can start to do this by first apologizing to him for not making him feel safe, by praising and appreciating him.

For example:

- I've noticed that we don't talk the way we used to, and I just want to apologize for not letting you be able to feel like you can talk to me about anything.

- Honey, I just wanted to tell you that I really appreciated you telling me about how you ran into your ex-girl friend the other day. It means a lot to me that you told me, instead of keeping it to yourself.

- Listen, I wanted to say that it's important for me to hear about what you are going through and what you think about. You let me go on and on about what I'm going through, and I want to hear about what you are dealing with.

As a 3rd, a wife is supposed to be his 'play-mate'. She makes herself sexually available to him. She knows his likes/dislikes in the bedroom. A 3rd study's him and isn't afraid to experiment and explore her partner. She knows how to seduce him (and he wants to be seduced). She doesn't deny him when he wants her. Along with seduction, she has more tricks up her sleeve to keep their bedroom time fresh and fun. She knows how to tease him. As a 3rd, she knows how to change her look to keep his eyes physically interested. Because women: men are always going to look. It's like they can't help but to look because they are so visually stimulated. So, work your magic so that he continues to look at you. Don't forget to do the kinds of things you did in the beginning of the relationship that kept it fresh and exciting. You know how women miss the "romance." Well, men also miss those feelings you made him feel in the beginning.

So, don't get too comfortable; every now and then mix things up. Buy yourself some lingerie to surprise him. Don't be afraid to go into the adult stores, or, if that is simply too much for you, stock up after Halloween with fun and flirty costumes. Now-a-days with the internet, you don't even have to deal with prying eyes; you can make your purchases totally in private. Go down to a hair store and get yourself a wig. Change your look. Go from brunette/blonde/red/pink/purple whatever color or length of hair. Be the same wife, but show him different women by role-playing. Totally surprise him by making a lunch date on a Friday and meet him incognito (wearing a new costume), flirt and have a great lunch and send him back to work excited to clock out at 5 p.m. to get back to you, his sexy wife.

If you are already married, look at your marriage. What areas are great? What areas need more development? Are you being a Main, 2nd, and 3rd? If not, then look at the roles you play in the marriage and see which area you need to develop. Sometimes life causes the drifts, but it might be the case that you have always acted as a Main and 2nd but not as a 3rd. Now that you are in a marriage, to keep it fresh and growing takes going into new levels to not become stagnant.

If you are not married, then be prepared to adapt once you are married to fulfill the Main, 2nd, and 3rd positions. Many times getting to the altar seems to be the pinnacle of dating. But once you are married, the real adventure begins.

From Price Tag To Priceless

Chapter Thirteen – Conclusion ~ My Story

I was in a relationship for 5 ½ years, and while I was in that relationship I was a Main, 2nd, and 3rd. In the beginning, I was a Main. We talked on the phone for about a month before we went on our first date which was the traditional movie and dinner. On our first date I met his mother, sister, and brother-in-law. After our first date, we went out to eat and hung out getting to know each other better. I made it clear that I was not ready to have sex and felt that it was something special, and he should know that up front. We dated for a few weeks then became "exclusive," going from dating to being "boyfriend/girlfriend". This title and level of commitment lasted for about two months then he broke up with me.

It seemed that the no sex part was an element that he had more trouble with then he thought he would have. One of his ex-girlfriends came by at the right place and time, and he had sex with her. So that he wouldn't have to tell me, and probably out of guilt, he decided to just break-up with me. After we had a few conversations, post break-up, he told me what he had done and why he broke-up with me.

The next weekend I went out to the club with my friends and there he was in line about five people in front of me. I had a choice to make. I could either: not talk to him and put him in my past because he had a problem with my no sex rule and he had cheated on me; or, I could play it cool like he never hurt me and walk up to him, say hello, and be nice. Well, I chose the latter.

It was pride. I chose my pride over wisdom. He had clearly told me, by his actions, that he was not ready or wanting to be in a celibate relationship and that he had issues with fidelity. Right then was the moment that I could have chosen to be wise and walk away from a situation that could cause me more hurt. Being prideful, I wanted him to know that he didn't break me. So I walked right up to him, tapped him on the shoulder, smiled and said hi. If I have known what taking this step would bring, I would have definitely chosen wisdom over pride. Taking this step dropped me out of my Main category into a 2nd and later a 3rd.

As archaic as it may sound, it is still true that men are the hunters! Had I chosen wisdom and let him go his way, and I go mine, he would have had to make the first move and work to get my attention. Instead, I took the initiative and spoke to him first. I didn't let him hunt. Because of my actions, going up to him, getting his attention, saying hello and being very pleasant, my category was then changed.

So, after taking this step of speaking to him, at first he was confused because there was no reason for me to be so nice after what he had done. But because I opened the lines of communication, I had given him the 'green light'.

He started calling me, and I was now a 2nd. He would talk about his future plans, and I would talk to him about mine. We would encourage each other and enjoy each others' company, but we were not committed to each other. We spent a good amount of time together just hanging out or working out together.

If we had just hung out and had no physical contact with each other, I would have stayed a 2nd, but that was not the case. Eventually, we did start to kiss, which progressed to making out and then sex, and I became a 3rd. Now, remember this all happened, and we weren't "boyfriend/girlfriend;" there was no commitment. All I had were feelings. These feelings came from how he made me feel, what he would say to me, and the attention he gave me.

Now, as I said before, this was a 5½ year relationship. But the thing about the category system is that your category changes based on your actions. The most important thing to know is that you control your category by the actions you take.

There were times that he would invite me to his family's home for parties and holidays, but sometimes he would pick me up to take me and other times he would just meet me there. The difference is important! If a man picks a woman up and takes her to this kind of event, he is telling everyone 'she's here with me'. If you meet up some place, he still has his freedom in which he will come by and talk to you, but, he's not obligated to leave with you, and you may not be the only person he invited to be there.

In addition to attending events with him and meeting him at events, we also went on dates, which complicated things even more. We would go out to eat, to the movies, to the park, and spend time sharing ourselves with each other. During this time, I wasn't seeing anyone else but him. He, however, did see other women. Because I chose to become invested in someone who was not exclusively seeing me, I wound up hurt - a lot! See, the thing is that hurt, hurts. Whether or not you have a semi-formal title like: "girlfriend" or "fiancé," and of course the formal title "wife", hurt hurts! So, during this period of time, I put myself through a massive amount of hurt. And every time I went back, I would give him another piece of me.

Eventually, I had given him so much of me that I was severely broken, emotionally and mentally! It was in this broken state that I found myself explaining and defending our involvement to my friends and family. I willingly gave him everything he wanted from me, and because of that, I fell deeper into the role of a 3rd. I threw myself into the situation and gave him the authority to set the parameters of our involvement.

The parameters that he set, and that I so passively agreed to, were that he didn't want to be in a committed relationship with me, but he still wanted to have me in his life. He told me he cared for me and that he never meant to hurt me. He said that he took actions that he wanted to take, but there was never an intention to cause me hurt. But because I invested so much in him, I accepted these terms, and when I would find out that he had been with other women, it hurt again. It was like I would hear what he said, but I would interpret it in such a different way. I interpreted what he said to what I wanted to hear.

I carefully choose my words above. I use the word "invested" instead of using the word "loved." The reason is this: you can't love another person without knowing how to love yourself. You see, accepting whatever he was willing to give me demonstrated how I didn't love myself. One reason is that, growing up, I didn't see real loving relationships. My parents got divorced after years of my father cheating on my mother. And I saw her take him back every time. I was also insecure about my looks. I had battled with my weight for years and didn't believe that I was attractive. I was used to being the "friend" but not the "girlfriend". I had guy friends but not a boyfriend. So, when he paid attention to me, it was an overwhelming feeling, and I enjoyed it. I was confident in other aspects of myself, but I didn't really love myself as a whole. And loving myself was what I was really lacking. I compensated the feeling of lack with outside things like food, alcohol, and being overly accommodating and compromising to make and keep friends. But none of these things could fill the void. When I finally got into a relationship, I gave it everything and it didn't work. I couldn't fix myself on the inside by distracting myself on the outside. And I really tried too. Over the course of 5½ years, I poured more of myself into a relationship and it caused me more damage than I could even imagine.

After being his 3rd for a few years, he met another woman, and a friend told me that he was seeing this woman pretty regularly. I was devastated and empty. I wanted some sort of validation that I was lovable. That someone could love me and make me his "girlfriend," that someone would choose me. Well, being at that low point, I was ready to hunt. I didn't want to wait to be found. Because waiting involved really looking at myself, it required me really admitting that I didn't love myself and that, if I didn't love me, who could? But after that initial question, I then had to find out why I didn't love myself and how to learn to love myself. And instead of taking the time to work on myself, I went back to the hunting ground – the clubs. I kept myself busy! I went out regularly, and when I was home I was on the phone. I dreaded being in silence because when it was quiet I would think. And I didn't really want to think about what I was doing and the consequences of it; I just wanted to "do". This phase lasted for a few months, but it really wasn't for me! After that period I was even emptier.

In this state of being hurt, I hurt myself: not physically, but definitely emotionally and mentally. Of course, I have to mention that throughout these phases I was going through, Mr. 5 ½ years would call me and see me from time to time, and I still played the 2nd or 3rd role with him. He was not committed to me and I was no longer committed to him, but I still cared for him in a way that I hadn't cared for any other man. Throughout our involvement, the last year was the most volatile one for the both of us. We hurt ourselves and each other a lot, and we caused each other so much pain.

Then one day we decided to try it again, for real this time, but taking it a bit slower. We stopped seeing other people and started hanging out and going out. Things were going great for a few weeks. Then he called and by the sound of his voice I knew I had to pull over and park the car to give this conversation my full attention. He explained that an old friend of his had called him and needed a ride home. He went and picked her up and took her home and they ended up having sex. I was crushed. My eyes welled up with tears, and they came pouring out. I couldn't believe it. Things had been going so well and I was truly caught off guard. So I told him that we couldn't be friends anymore and that I wished him well, but I told him that I didn't want him to ever call me again.

After we hung up, I sat crying in my car, and then I began to pray. It went something like this, "God, I can't believe I'm in this situation again! But this time, God, I need your help. Please help me! Please forgive me for doing things I know I shouldn't have done. I'm sorry. I don't want to be in a relationship anymore. The next time I am in a relationship, I want it to be Your timing, not mine. I want him to be Your choice for me. But until then, I want to be dedicated to You. I want You to be the one I love. Teach me to love myself. I want to serve You and not get distracted by anything or anyone. I want to be committed to

You. I need it to be just You and me for a while. And please help him. I don't want to hate him; help me to forgive him. I want him to have a good life, even if it's not with me. I love You, God ~ Amen."

    I wiped my tears, took a few deep breaths and felt better. I drove back to work and had a good day. It was strange, but I felt good. I started spending more time developing my relationship with God. I prayed every night and read my Bible everyday and felt surprisingly fulfilled. I noticed little things that would happen throughout the days that helped me, like hearing great songs on the radio that made me smile. It was easy for the first time in over 5 years to be without him. He was no longer part of my daily life, but I wasn't really missing him. Every day was better than the last. I continued to grow stronger and started to look back at how I had allowed myself to get lost in the relationship. I started to work on myself and after having prayed, I didn't have that empty feeling that I had before. Things were going well, and I just felt new and refreshed.

After praying that day in my car, I carried myself as, and was treated as, a treasure. I became a wife and have incorporated all three roles within my marriage. In public, I'm a Main. In our daily life together with him I'm a 2nd. And in the bedroom, I know how to be a 3rd!

It was a painful lesson to learn, but the journey taught me that I determine my value. I decide how I will be treated. Once you truly know your worth, why would you settle for anything less?

My hope is that after reading this book, you will take the time to heal yourself. Discover your value. Develop into the person you aspire to be, and when you aren't looking, he will find you. He will see your character and follow the map, he will seek, dig, discover, recover, open the chest and treasure you.

THE END

Adriana Ivett Petty graduated from Saint Mary's College in Notre Dame, Indiana in 2001, earning her bachelors degree in social work with a minor in anthropology. Adriana is originally from McAllen, Texas but currently resides in South Bend, Indiana with her husband, Joseph Lee Petty.

Made in the USA
Middletown, DE
19 January 2016